New World Provence

Good Food
Good Life

Jean Frue

Happy Cooking

Bon Appétit!

Alessandra

New World Provence

MODERN FRENCH COOKING FOR FRIENDS AND FAMILY

Alessandra and Jean-Francis Quaglia

ARSENAL
PULP PRESS

VANCOUVER

NEW WORLD PROVENCE

Copyright © 2007 by Alessandra and Jean-Francis Quaglia

2nd printing: 2008

ARSENAL PULP PRESS
341 Water Street, Suite 200
Vancouver, BC
Canada V6B 1B8
arsenalpulp.com

The publisher gratefully acknowledges the support of the Government of Canada through the Book
Publishing Industry Development Program and the Government of British Columbia through the Book
Publishing Tax Credit Program for its publishing activities.

The authors and publisher assert that the information contained in this book is true and complete
to the best of their knowledge. All recommendations are made without guarantee on the part of the
authors and publisher. The authors and publisher disclaim any liability in connection with the use of this
information. For more information, contact the publisher.

Text and cover design by Electra Design Group
Edited by Bethanne Grabham
Food and selected B&W photographs by Hamid Attie
Other photographs courtesy of the authors
Front cover food images (left to right):
    Roasted Sweet Potatoes (page 103)
    Fresh Tomato Tarte (page 48)
    Pear & Fig Tarte (page 185)

Printed and bound in China

Library and Archives Canada Cataloguing in Publication:
Quaglia, Alessandra, 1968-

    New World Provence : modern French cooking for friends and family /
    Alessandra and Jean-Francis Quaglia.

Includes index.
ISBN 978-1-55152-223-4

    1. Cookery, French. I. Quaglia, Jean-Francis, 1968- II. Title.
TX719.Q83 2007   641.5944   C2007-904446-8

Contents

We would like to dedicate this book to our sons Remi and Matisse

whose discerning palates keep us on our toes!

Acknowledgments

....

Firstly we would like to thank our mothers Jette and Suzanne and stepmother Dorothy. They are forever strong and loving, and continue to support us, unconditionally.

Thanks to our dad and father-in-law Nicholas Mossa for getting us started and helping us to realize our dream.

Thank you, Remi and Matisse, for your patience during the production of this book.

Our photographer and dear friend Hamid Attie put his heart and soul into every picture and we are so grateful and thrilled with the outcome.

Our utmost appreciation goes to Del for stepping in to relieve our anxiety and help us organize all the recipes.

Thank you to all our wonderful and dedicated staff who make it possible for us to actually have a life, unlike many other restaurateurs.

It has been a great experience working with everyone at Arsenal Pulp. Special thanks to Bethanne Grabham for her patience throughout the editing process.

A very special shout out to all our friends and family, with whom we enjoy sharing many great meals.

Finally, we are extremely grateful to our clientele for supporting us over the last ten years. You keep our mission alive.

FOREWORD BY DOMINIQUE LESTANC

....

I remember the first time I met Jean-Francis Quaglia. He wanted me to hire him at the Hôtel Negresco in Nice, France, one of the most renowned hotels in the world. At the time, I was *chef de cuisine* at the hotel's restaurant, which had two Michelin stars. Jean-Francis was only in his early twenties, but I could tell he was talented with a strong character, dedicated to his chosen career with help from his mother, chef Suzanne Quaglia, and her restaurant Le Patalain in Marseille. He studied at L'Ecole Hôtelière there, and also trained at other famed restaurants, such as Le Chevre D'Or in Eze, close to Nice. He made a very favorable first impression on me, so I hired him right away, a decision which I would not regret. I saw very quickly that he was a real cook and I felt that he would go far; he was showing the necessary application and inspiration, and a real passion for his craft. At an age when most young people are easily distracted, Jean-Francis always paid very close attention to the fine details. After several weeks on the job, he became *chef de partie tournant*, having full responsibility for each station in the kitchen, such as fish, meat, and vegetables.

Then one day a young Canadian from Toronto named Alessandra, who had just finished cooking school, knocked on my door to ask for an apprenticeship in my kitchen, saying she wanted to perfect her knowledge of French cuisine, specifically Meridional (i.e. the South of France). I felt that she was determined enough, so I agreed to hire her. I noticed right away that our *stagiere* Alessandra and our chef de partie Jean-Francis seemed to share the same passion for their work. Their chemistry flourished and soon they were never apart.

After leaving the Negresco and then spending some more time in Marseille, they thought they would try their luck in Canada, Alessandra's native country. There they enhanced their cooking expertise amidst a huge variety of cuisines without ever forgetting their love for Provençal fine dining. Five years later, in 1997, they opened their first restaurant, Provence Mediterranean Grill in Vancouver, bringing their love for French flavors to local customers, who quickly took note. Shortly after opening, they received the Gold Award for best bistro from *Vancouver Magazine*. In the meantime, they also started to build a family, resulting in two sons.

A few years later, they opened a second restaurant in Vancouver, Provence Marinaside, giving the city another opportunity to appreciate some truly Mediterranean specialties, such as the famous Marseillaise bouillabaisse with *rouille* and croutons as well as a warm goat cheese salad with *herbes de Provence*. They also served the legendary *pissaladière*, and one of his mother's specialties, grilled quail with juniper berries.

I believe Jean-Francis and Alessandra owe their success to their conviction in the foods and methods of Provençal cooking, a cuisine rich with flavor and color. A true cuisine does not exist without tradition, but neither can it exist without being open to innovation. Jean-Francis and Alessandra understand this, and as a result, their craft and talent shine. They prove it with dishes such as their succulent prawns sautéed with extra virgin olive oil and served with a *socca galette* and tomatoes. (In Nice, socca is still enjoyed today as a snack by early morning workers and tourists; it is a large crêpe made from chickpea flour, cooked in a fire wood oven, where the crêpe is browned to the point that its surface looks burnt, like a woman who spends too much time at the beach!)

Each one of Jean-Francis and Alessandra's dishes manage to reveal and procure deep culinary pleasure. With this book, they want to share their love for and dedication to Provençal food with those who have been enchanted by their restaurants and wish to bring that experience home to their own dinner table, as well as those who may have never visited their premises but wish to know more about the traditions (both old and new) of Provençal cuisine.

The rest is up to readers of this book as they follow the simple yet precise recipes the Quaglias offer here. For those who are new to French cooking: know that everything is possible as long as you remember this quote by Anthelme Brillat-Savarin, a French lawyer and politician who was quite possibly the most famous epicure and gastronome in all of France during the eighteenth century: "Of all the qualities of a cook, the most indispensable is their accuracy."

To everyone, I wish you many delicious discoveries and *un trés bon appétit!*

—*Dominique LeStanc*
Chef and owner, La Merenda restaurant
Nice, France
July 2007

FOREWORD BY ROB FEENIE

....

People in the restaurant business are very passionate and pour every ounce of their energy into their work, but at the same time, they strive to maintain personal lives outside of their hectic schedules. I cannot think of two people who can balance both worlds better than my very good friends, Jean-Francis and Alessandra. They have two amazing restaurants, Provence Mediterranean Grill and Provence Marinaside, and two amazing children, Remi and Matisse. Both Jean-Francis and Alessandra bring a very proud family spirit to both of their establishments, which showcase the culture and cuisine of the South of France right here in Vancouver. Jean-Francis and I first met in the early 1990s at the French bistro Chez Thierry on Robson Street in Vancouver; he had just arrived here in Canada from France. A few years later, in 1995, when I opened my restaurant Lumière, we crossed paths again through my sous chef, Frank Pabst, who had worked with Jean-Francis at the Hôtel Negresco in Nice—what an extraordinary place to meet! As a result, Jean-Francis and I renewed our friendship that included great food (of course), great wine, and most importantly, our families.

Jean-Francis and Alessandra opened their first Provence restaurant on West 10th Avenue in Vancouver in December 1997, and I can remember it like it was yesterday. Frank and I arrived after work to share a celebratory glass of wine with Jean-Francis and Alessandra and to get a taste of their first menu—and to this day, I return to that restaurant weekly for more. I once had a staff party for Lumière and we served almost every item from Provence's antipasti menu, including the pissaladière and merguez sausage; the food was amazing, a truly unforgettable culinary experience for the staff. I also can never get enough of their classic fish soup; in fact, anything they create with seafood is fantastic because their ingredients are so simple—a little olive oil, lemon juice, white wine, sometimes a hint of butter—and prepared in ways that are understated yet sophisticated at the same time. My all-time favorite entrée is the roasted free-run chicken Provençal; I do not know how many times I have had it, but I can never get enough—it is the perfect meal, especially when accompanied by a simple sauce and grilled vegetables. Another two of my favorites are the wild mushroom ravioli and the crab, prawn, and scallop open ravioli with the creamy lobster bisque. These are just a few of my picks, as Provence's food is always so damn good.

I believe any great restaurant must have passion and soul in the kitchen. The reason that Jean-Francis and Alessandra have been so successful is because they possess both of these qualities, and more. The South of France has always been a special place for me, with its warm, sunny weather and great food. I believe it is one of the most magical places in all of Europe. Let this book take you on a wonderful journey there. *Bon appétit!*

—Rob Feenie
Chef and owner, Lumière and Feenie's restaurants
Vancouver, Canada
August 2007

INTRODUCTION

....

ALESSANDRA: I never quite knew what I wanted to be when I grew up. Dreams of becoming a ballerina were wiped out after an unsuccessful audition for the National Ballet of Canada. And I was always more of a social bunny than an academic at school, so any lofty aspirations of becoming a lawyer were quickly dashed. Cooking, however, was always a secret passion.

My Danish mother and Italian father are both first-generation Canadians and both had very strong ties to family. I grew up in Toronto with my sister and mom. My parents divorced when I was three, so holidays and weekends were often split to accommodate both sides of the family. During many a weekend visit with my Danish grandparents at Sunset Villa, a community property enjoyed by Danes in Guelph, Ontario, I would often watch my Mormor ("mother's mom" in Danish) and my Möster (mother's aunt) create beautiful Danish buffets called *smörgåsbord*, a name that is also used in English (directly translated, it means "buttered bread"). These buffets usually consist of cold roast beef, roast pork, and fish, plus lots of different condiments so guests can make their own sandwiches. I used to love watching my Mormor create specialty open-faced sandwiches that were truly works of art; my favorite was the liver pâté with cucumber salad or sliced beets on Danish rye bread.

On other Sundays, I visited my Nonna and Nonno, my Italian grandparents. My Nonna and Zia (great aunt) Rocky would always be hard at work in the kitchen creating wonderful Italian meals that started at noon and continued into the evening. We always had some type of seafood, like squid or mussels and clams, then some pasta with a homemade sauce; lamb roasted on the barbecue was usually the main entrée. My fondest memory was always the end of the meal, when all my cousins and I would eagerly await for the home-made *zabaliogne*, a dessert made with egg yolks and sugar and served in small espresso cups.

Good food was certainly a natural part of my genetic makeup. My interest in it flourished when my dad, who was a hairdresser, needed a new challenge and opened his first restaurant called Blondies (after his daughters!), a few doors down from his hair salon on Yonge Street in Toronto. He always worked closely with the chefs, and it wasn't long before I began taking notes. One day when my dad and I were in the kitchen, I noticed his proficient chopping skills, and I asked him to show me how. Holding that chef's knife and trying desperately to emulate his method was a turning point for me—when my secret passion became a real career choice.

After graduating from high school in 1987, my mother bought me a plane ticket to spend the summer in Denmark. Unknowingly, she had planted the travel bug in me. One summer turned into a year, during which I worked as a breakfast cook at the Hotel Admiral in Copenhagen. I loved the ambiance in the kitchen there. Upon returning to Toronto after my year away, I immediately applied to the Culinary Management program at the George Brown School of Hospitality. After my first year, I was anxious to get out in the field to work.

My boyfriend at the time had family with property in Nice, France, and every summer he would spend a month there. I had always dreamt of visiting the South of France, and in May 1990, at the age of twenty-two, I flew to Europe on my own again, this time to Nice. With the help of my boyfriend's family and friends, I was able to make some connections regarding a cooking apprenticeship. The plan was for me to work for a couple months before he arrived in August for his vacation. There were only two things that complicated my quest: I needed a working visa and I would have to find restaurants that accepted women in the kitchen. Back in the early 1990s, women were not yet taken seriously in the male-dominated industry. One restaurant bluntly refused my application, proudly stating that they simply did not allow women to work there. My other option was to apply as a *stagiere*, or apprentice, by which one worked for free at various restaurants and gained experience by watching and doing small jobs for two to three weeks at a time. At each kitchen I worked, there were anywhere from six to sixteen male cooks around me. I tried to stay focused, because after all my main goal was to learn as much as I could about fine French food, but needless to say, I got distracted and my relationship with my boyfriend was doomed.

I was very fortunate to work with some great French chefs, including Jacques Maximin, Bruno Caironi, Jean-Jacques Jouteux, and Dominique LeStanc. Dominique, from Chantecler at the Hôtel Negresco, was the one who ended up giving me the chance of a lifetime by sponsoring me for a three-month work visa, which allowed me to work more seriously as a *commis de cuisine* and focus on a specific station in the kitchen. I recall my third day of official work at Chantecler, when I had been chopping all sorts of onions and trying to be stoic about it. In a kitchen of fifteen male cooks, there was no way I could show any sort of vulnerability. I remember looking up from the misery of my task and there he was, unbeknownst to me my future husband, Jean-Francis, looking straight into my presumably reddened eyes. He gestured with a nod to say hello. No words were exchanged but right then and there we had an instant attraction. Our conversations were limited due to the fact that neither of us could speak the other's language, but I must say, the language of love is universal.

JEAN-FRANCIS: For as long as I can remember, I have always been exposed to fine French cuisine. My mother, lovingly known as Mamie Suzanne, is a voracious cook. Even though she was a single mom—my father died in a tragic car accident when I was only ten months old—she entertained friends and family almost every weekend while I was growing up. She would take my brother Jacques and me to wonderful restaurants whenever we traveled outside of Marseille, where we lived. It was therefore inevitable that food became a passion for me very early. At the age of eight, I began experimenting with pastries, and my lemon tarte quickly became a favorite amongst our dinner guests. When I turned twelve, my mother felt I needed more of a male influence in my life, so she sent me to spend time with my Tonton (uncle) Pierrot and Tatie (aunt) Josette at their traditional *boulangerie* (bakery) in the small Haute Provence village of Forqualquier. My uncle started work at eleven o'clock each night to prepare the next day's baked goods to be sold in their store. I was ambitious and wanted to help him, figuring it would give me a taste of the life of a real baker. However, by three in the morning, my uncle would usually find me snoozing on a big bag of flour. My mother advised me that the life of a *boulanger* was not conducive to healthy family life and encouraged me to take the route of *chef cuisinier* instead.

When I was fourteen, my mother took over a twenty-seat restaurant called Le Patalain (the previous owners were named Patricia and Alain, hence the name). At the age of sixteen, I enrolled in a culinary program that would last two years. Le Patalain was an exciting place for me to practice my skills while learning the trade. I was able to see first-hand what was involved in running a small business. Soon, however, the restaurant became too small for my mother, whom the people of Marseille now referred to as "La Mère Marseillaise." She moved the business closer to the Vieux Port (the Old Port) where she built her dream restaurant. Retaining the name, the new establishment was definitely Michelin-star quality with all the bells and whistles. My brother managed the front of the house while she oversaw the kitchen. After fifteen years, my mother became respected as one of the best female chefs in Marseille, and received the coveted La Clef D'Or award from Gault et Millaud, amongst many other accolades.

After graduating, my mother suggested I further my culinary education by going to work for *des bonnes maisons* ("some great restaurants"). I started at the Hôtel Sofitel Vieux Port in Marseille, which gave me good experience in traditional French cuisine. I then moved on to the Côte D'Azur, where I landed a job at the reputable La Chevre D'Or in Eze Village. It was commonplace for young cooks to move around after one season to get as much exposure to different chefs as possible. I then moved on to Chantecler in the famed Hôtel Negresco in Nice. As far as cooking was concerned, Dominique LeStanc of Chantecler became a major influence on me in the way I wanted to express myself with food, and on a personal level, it was there at Chantecler that my life's fortune would be determined. After meeting Alessandra, we started a relationship that changed my life forever.

ALESSANDRA: Jean-Francis and I both reminisce regularly about those wonderful days in France. Sometimes we look at the letters we sent each other during the nine months after I had returned to Toronto, not knowing if we'd ever see each other again, but something told me that I needed to figure out if we could seriously have a future together. I returned to Nice in April of 1991 and shortly thereafter followed Jean-Francis back to his hometown. Together we worked with Mamie Suzanne at Le Patalain, where I quickly became fluent in French and learned to appreciate and love Provençal cooking and the French way of life. After a year of living and working together seven days a week, we knew that marriage was on our life's menu! Appeasing my mother and her request that we return to Toronto to marry, we exchanged vows on May 23, 1992.

After our wedding, we decided to take my father up on his offer to fly us out to Vancouver where he lived and contemplate the idea of opening a restaurant there. Being newly married, it seemed like the natural thing to do, starting fresh in a new city. Shortly after we arrived the brain-storming began; my father and my stepmother Dorothy were the major investors, and offered many interesting ideas. However, we soon hit a brick wall when we couldn't seem to agree on one concept. My father wanted a casual Italian bistro and we wanted a fine, Michelin star-quality establishment; after all, we had just arrived from Europe with training from some of the best restaurants in France. Our visions were at opposite ends of the spectrum, but perhaps in the end it was a blessing in disguise. It would be five years until our ideas would finally come together and Provence was born. During those five years, Jean-Francis and I were able to meet and get to know the people of Vancouver and learn about the eating habits of West Coasters; we realized that for the most part Vancouverites had a casual but well-educated palate, not unlike other North American cities.

The story of how we found our first location is one I'll never forget. One sunny day in July, Jean-Francis went out to buy fertilizer for our garden. He was gone longer than expected, and when he finally pulled up in the driveway, he hurried us all back into the car, including our roommate Frank Pabst and his fiancée Kelley. Jean-Francis was so excited and told us we had to see what he had just discovered on his shopping trip. We soon arrived on West 10th Avenue in the Point Grey neighborhood, in front of a dilapidated old building with a small sign in the window that read "For Lease."

Despite its condition, Jean-Francis and I both thought it would be the perfect place for our restaurant. After much negotiation with the landlord, we soon secured the lease in our name and six months later opened Provence Mediterranean Grill. The neighborhood welcomed our arrival; the restuarant was busy from day one. We offered a simple menu with dishes representative of the South of France, in a casual atmosphere that was warm and inviting. Items such as our Warm Goat Cheese Salad (page 45), Prawns Provençal (page 131) with butter, garlic and flambéed with brandy, and Roast Chicken with Herbes de Provence (page 148) quickly became staples that locals would come back two or three times a week to order. Four years later, we took another leap of faith and opened a second restaurant, Provence Marinaside in the Yaletown district of Vancouver. Sadly, our home garden died due to the lack of fertilizer, but we've never looked back.

More than fifteen years, two kids, and two restaurants later, I am still inspired by Jean-Francis's love and dedication to his craft and his family. We still share a deep passion for food together and often share that passion with our friends and family. Our cooking philosophy has ultimately been formed by the female figures in both our lives. My mother would always amaze us by the way she would come home after a long day at work and manage to make dinner out of what looked like an empty fridge, which has given me the skill to also prepare meals *à la minute*. And Jean-Francis's mom gave him the confidence to go forth and hone his skills by passing on to him her undying passion for real Provençal cooking.

Together we create good simple meals with fresh seasonal ingredients that often take us back to our respective childhoods, but at the same time we also enjoy experimenting with different foods and creating new recipes. We are both quite adamant about the way we teach our children how to eat. In today's world of processed foods, we make a conscious effort to feed them only what is fresh and authentically flavorful. Generally, we never make separate "kids' food" for our sons; we cook meals for our entire family, whether adult or child. It's not always easy, but I can honestly say that we are raising two of the most educated "foodies" who are always willing to try new dishes. The rule in our house is, "You are allowed NOT to like it but you are not allowed to NOT try it," because ultimately your enjoyment of cooking will come from your loved ones' enjoyment of eating what you cook. So keep it simple and fresh, and don't be afraid to try something new.

We hope that in some ways we have changed the way people think of French food. Provence is a region full of color, sunshine, and simple yet robust tastes. Our dishes show how French food can be light (and good for you) without compromising flavor: garlic, extra virgin olive oil, tomatoes, and fresh herbs come together to enhance fresh fish and poultry, while beef tenderloin simply studded with garlic and served with sautéed French beans will satisfy the most discerning of carnivores. Thankfully, the West Coast lends itself well to the needs of the Provençal chef, with an abundance of fresh fish and local farms. That is what our cooking is all about; and although many of these recipes are precise, which can be helpful for the amateur cook, we would encourage you to experiment to suit your individual food preferences and cooking style.

This book represents a lifetime of our love for food, the West Coast, and each other. We continue to share our joy every day with our dear clientele and with precious friends and family. We're also pleased to include some favorite recipes of Mamie Suzanne, who always captures the hearts of those she meets during her numerous visits to Vancouver, where she often works in our restaurants' kitchens, sharing her passion for the art of cooking and good food—something we hope to share with you too, through this book.

Antipasti

Sautéed Squid with Chili-Citrus
Vinaigrette

Stewed Squid
in Tomato Saffron Sauce

Snapper Escabeche

Pissaladière (Caramelized Onion
Thin Crust Pizza)

Coco Bean & Wild Mushroom Ragoût

Ratatouille

Roasted Vegetables Tossed in Pesto

Grilled Mushrooms

Roasted Red Bell Peppers

Fennel à l'Orange

Roasted Chicken
with Olives & Garlic Confit

Merguez Sausage

Sautéed Squid with Chili-Citrus Vinaigrette

Squid has a wonderful texture but needs strong flavors to help it along. Our son Remi loves this dish and eats it every chance he gets. Don't forget to have some crusty baguette on hand to sop up the sauce!

Separate squid tubes from tentacles with a knife. On both sides of each squid tube, make three small vertical cuts one-third of the way down. Place squid tubes in a bowl, season with salt and pepper, and drizzle with 2 tbsp oil. In a frying pan on high heat, add squid tubes and sauté for about 1 minute on each side, until just cooked. Remove from pan and set aside. In the same frying pan on high, heat another 1 tbsp oil. Add squid tentacles and sear for 30 seconds on each side. Remove from pan and set aside. In the same frying pan on medium-high heat, add another 1 tbsp oil. Add garlic and sauté for 1 minute. Add chili flakes and Tabasco and Worcestershire sauces and stir to combine. Return squid tubes and tentacles to pan, drizzle with lemon juice and remaining 1 tbsp oil, and cook for an additional 2–3 minutes, but no longer; it is very important not to overcook squid. Sprinkle parsley over top and serve.

MAKES 4 SERVINGS.

FRESH SQUID CAN BE PURCHASED AT YOUR LOCAL SEAFOOD MARKET. IF FRESH SQUID IS NOT AVAILABLE, YOU MAY SUBSTITUTE WITH FROZEN, WHICH IS AVAILABLE FROM AT MOST SUPERMARKETS.

1 lb (455 g) fresh squid tubes and tentacles, cleaned (see note)

Salt to taste

Freshly ground black pepper to taste

4 tbsp extra virgin olive oil

1 tbsp garlic, chopped

1 tsp chili flakes

Tabasco sauce to taste

Worcestershire sauce to taste

Juice of 1 large lemon

¼ cup fresh parsley, chopped

STEWED SQUID IN TOMATO SAFFRON SAUCE

....

4 tbsp olive oil

1 lb (455 g) small baby squid tubes and tentacles, cleaned (see note)

Salt to taste

Freshly ground black pepper to taste

¼ medium onion, chopped

3 cloves garlic, chopped

3 cups Tomato Sauce (page 87)

¼ tsp saffron threads

Fresh parsley, chopped (for garnish)

Always be careful not to overcook squid, otherwise it will be as if you are chewing rubber! This recipe can be made in advance, but make sure to only partially cook the squid so it can cook through when reheating.

Separate squid tubes from tentacles with a knife and score tubes. In a frying pan on high, heat 2 tbsp oil. Briefly sear squid, cooking through only halfway, then remove immediately. Place in a bowl, season with salt and pepper, and set aside. In the same pan on medium, heat an additional 2 tbsp oil. Add onions and garlic and sauté to sweat for about 2–3 minutes. Add tomato sauce and saffron, reduce heat, and simmer for 5 minutes so saffron can be absorbed. Before adding squid to sauce, strain squid of any excess water released during the cooking process. Add squid to tomato sauce and cook for an additional 2–3 minutes, until squid is just cooked; it is very important not to overcook it. Check for seasoning. Garnish with parsley and serve warm.

MAKES 4 SERVINGS.

FRESH BABY SQUID CAN BE PURCHASED AT YOUR LOCAL FISH MARKET. IF FRESH SQUID IS NOT AVAILABLE, YOU MAY SUBSTITUTE WITH FROZEN, WHICH IS AVAILABLE AT MOST SUPERMARKETS.

SNAPPER ESCABECHE

....

Although this recipe hails from Spain, it is very popular in Provence. Traditionally, escabeche is a mixture of vinegar, oil, herbs, and seasonings used to preserve or "pickle" foods such as poultry, fish, chilies, and vegetables. We often serve this as an antipasti but it can also be served cold as an appetizer.

In a bowl, combine salt and pepper. In a large sauté pan on medium-high, heat 2 tbsp oil. Season fish with salt-pepper mixture and place on pan to sear for 3 minutes on each side, then transfer to a plate and set aside. Heat remaining 1 tbsp oil in pan, add onions and garlic, and sauté for 2 minutes. Add wine and vinegar, and let liquid reduce by half, stirring occasionally. Add tomatoes and stir to combine. Add bay leaves and thyme, stir, and reduce heat to simmer for another 10 minutes. Return fish to pan and cook for another 5 minutes. Serve on a large platter and sprinkle with fresh herbs.

MAKES 4 SERVINGS.

1 tsp salt

1 tsp black pepper

3 tbsp extra virgin olive oil

4 pieces (6-oz/170-g each) snapper

1 medium white onion, sliced

1 tbsp garlic, chopped

¼ cup white wine

¼ cup sherry vinegar

1 can (13½-oz/400-mL) plum tomatoes, chopped (about 1¾ cups)

3 bay leaves

1 sprig fresh thyme

½ cup fresh herbs (e.g., chives, basil, parsley), chopped

Pissaladière (Caramelized Onion Thin Crust Pizza)

....

DOUGH (to be prepared the night before):

1½ cups + 3 tbsp (375 mL) water (room temperature)

1 tbsp fresh yeast (or 1 tsp dried yeast)

1 tbsp sugar

¼ cup pale ale beer (do not use dark beer)

1 tbsp + 2 tsp salt

3¼ cups flour

¼ cup olive oil

5 onions, thinly sliced

1 tsp herbes de Provence (see note)

3 cloves garlic, chopped

Salt to taste

Freshly ground black pepper to taste

Extra virgin olive oil (to coat baking sheet)

8 anchovy filets

15 fresh whole Kalamata olives, pitted (do not substitute with canned olives)

This French-style pizza is another one of those recipes that really brings you back to the South of France. The combination of the sweet onions, flavorful olives, and salty anchovies are a match made in heaven! Serve warm, with a high acid, fruity red or white wine.

TO PREPARE DOUGH: In a bowl, combine water, yeast, and sugar and mix. When yeast becomes frothy, add beer and stir to combine. Stir in salt and flour until well combined. On a lightly floured surface, knead dough into a ball. Cover with plastic wrap and refrigerate overnight. The next day, remove dough from fridge and let it return to room temperature.

TO PREPARE PISSALADIÈRE: Preheat oven to 375°F (190°C). In large frying pan on medium, heat oil. Add onions, herbes de Provence, garlic, salt, and pepper and sauté for 30 minutes, until onions caramelize. Remove from heat and allow mixture to cool for 15–20 minutes. Cut ball of dough in half, saving the remainder in a sealed container in the refrigerator or freezer to use at another time. Rub a cookie sheet with extra virgin olive oil. Roll out dough evenly and place on cookie sheet. Poke dough with a fork to prevent bubbling. Spread onion mixture evenly over top, then arrange anchovies in a criss-cross pattern and dot with olives. Bake for 20–25 minutes, or until crust turns golden.

MAKES 4 SERVINGS (WHEN CUT INTO 6 LARGE SLICES), OR MORE FOR APPETIZERS (WHEN CUT IN 12 SMALLER SLICES).

HERBES DE PROVENCE IS A TRADITIONAL BLEND OF DRIED HERBS COLLECTED FROM THE HILLS OF SOUTHERN FRANCE IN THE SUMMER. A TYPICAL BAG WILL CONSIST OF MARJORAM, OREGANO, ROSEMARY, SUMMER SAVORY, BAY LEAVES, AND THYME. LAVENDER IS ALSO INCLUDED OCCASIONALLY. HERBES DE PROVENCE CAN BE PURCHASED AT GOURMET OR SPECIALTY MARKETS, OR COMBINE THEM ON YOUR OWN.

Coco Bean & Wild Mushroom Ragoût

....

This is comfort food at its best; prepare it when the bounty of wild mushrooms are in season.

In a sauté pan on medium-high heat, melt butter. Add mushrooms and sauté for about 5 minutes, until brown on one side. Add onions, garlic, thyme, and bay leaf and sauté for about 2 minutes, until all liquid is absorbed. Deglaze with white wine and chicken stock. Add coco beans and bring to a simmer for 15–20 minutes. Remove herbs and serve.

Makes 4 servings.

The coco bean is a white bean that is similar in taste and appearance to the navy bean but smaller. Coco beans are available in gourmet or specialty markets. If you are using dried beans, remember to soak them overnight and cook them before using. Feel free to use white navy beans or any type of dried legume in place of the coco beans.

2 tbsp butter

2 cups wild mushrooms (e.g., shiitake, Portobello, chanterelle), larger ones sliced

¼ medium onion, chopped

2 cloves garlic, minced

1 sprig fresh thyme

1 bay leaf

¼ cup white wine

½ cup chicken stock

1 can (13-oz/398-mL) coco beans, drained and rinsed (see note)

RATATOUILLE

1 cup olive oil

4 small–medium onions, chopped

4–5 large cloves of garlic, chopped

4 red bell peppers, seeded and cubed

2 lb (1 kg) fresh ripe tomatoes, seeded and cubed

1 bay leaf

1 pinch sugar

6 small zucchini, sliced in quarters lengthwise and cubed

Salt to taste

Freshly ground black pepper to taste

3 small eggplants, sliced in quarters lengthwise and cubed

Fresh parsley or basil, chopped (for garnish)

The key to preparing this delicious Provençal vegetable ragoût is cooking the vegetables separately, then once they have been combined, allowing the ingredients to simmer long enough for all the flavors to blend (it tastes even better the next day and doesn't necessarily need to be heated up). This recipe calls for a sauteuse, *a round, lidded pot with small handles on each side, rather than a conventional, single straight-handled cooking pot. Sauteuses are commonly used in European household kitchens to sauté or braise a variety of foods and cook casseroles, stews, and pasta dishes. If you don't have a sauteuse, simply use any cooking pot you would use for a stew.*

In a large sauteuse (or pot) on medium, heat ¼ cup oil. Add onions and sauté, allowing them to sweat for about 3 minutes, until almost translucent. Add garlic and peppers and sauté for 3–4 minutes, until they begin to brown. Add tomatoes, bay leaf, and sugar. Stir mixture and simmer on medium heat until most of the liquid evaporates. Meanwhile, in a frying pan on medium, heat another ¼ cup oil. Add zucchini, season with salt and pepper, and sauté for 3–4 minutes, until they begin to brown. Add zucchini to other ingredients in sauteuse. Place the same pan used for zucchini on medium-high to heat an additional ¼ cup oil. Add eggplant (it may absorb oil quickly so you may need to add more oil). Season with salt and pepper and sauté until eggplant is soft. Add eggplant to other ingredients in sauteuse and simmer on medium heat for about 20 minutes. Check for seasoning before serving. Serve in a large bowl or platter, or even better, straight from the pan onto plates. Garnish with parsley or basil.

MAKES 8 SERVINGS.

ROASTED VEGETABLES TOSSED IN PESTO

....

Great as an antipasti or side dish, the pesto adds pizazz to otherwise simple roasted vegetables. Serve fresh from the oven.

TO PREPARE PESTO: In a food processor, add basil, cheese, garlic, and pine nuts and purée, while gradually adding oil, to form a smooth purée. Season with salt and pepper and set aside.

Preheat oven to 425°F (220°C). Ideally, each type of vegetable should be roasted separately, but if you have limited oven space and/or roasting pans, you can roast some of them together—for example, carrots, onion, fennel, and garlic; eggplant and mushrooms; bell peppers; and zucchini, which should be roasted separately or added last, as it cooks the fastest. Place vegetables in roasting pans, season liberally with salt and pepper, and drizzle with oil. Roast for 12–15 minutes, except zucchini, which requires 8–10 minutes, so turn them and check often to avoid burning. Once vegetables are softened, remove from oven and combine in a large bowl. Add pesto and stir until vegetables are well coated.

MAKES 4 SERVINGS.

PESTO:

2 cups fresh basil leaves, packed

½ cup freshly grated Romano cheese (or Parmesan)

6 medium cloves garlic, minced

⅓ cup pine nuts

½ cup extra virgin olive oil

Salt to taste

Freshly ground black pepper to taste

2 large carrots, cut in large pieces

1 Spanish (red) onion, cut into 6-8 wedges

1 fennel bulb, cut in large pieces

1 bulb garlic, separated into cloves and peeled

1 medium eggplant, cut in large pieces

1 cup button mushrooms

½ red bell pepper, seeded and cut in large pieces

½ yellow bell pepper, seeded and cut in large pieces

1 zucchini, cut in large pieces

Salt to taste

Freshly ground black pepper to taste

½ cup olive oil

GRILLED MUSHROOMS

....

¼ cup Worcestershire sauce

¼ cup Tabasco sauce

2 tbsp butter

1 clove garlic, minced

½ cup white wine

6 cups water

4 Portobello mushrooms, de-stemmed

2 cups button mushrooms

2 cups oyster mushrooms

¼ cup olive oil

¼ cup fresh parsley, chopped

1 tbsp extra virgin olive oil (for finishing)

1 tbsp balsamic vinegar (for finishing)

This recipe has become a staple on our restaurant's antipasti menu. For those who love mushrooms it's a sure pleaser. Generally, you can find these mushrooms fresh year-round in grocery stores; however, feel free to try substituting with different types in the fall, during peak mushroom season.

In a large pot on high heat, combine Worcestershire and Tabasco sauces, butter, garlic, wine, and water, and bring to a boil. Once boiling, add all mushrooms and cook for about 6 minutes, stirring frequently so mushrooms cook evenly. Strain, place mushrooms in a bowl, and toss with oil. In a stovetop grill pan on high heat (ensure the pan is hot), grill mushrooms in batches for about 2 minutes on each side, until they have defined grill marks. (Alternatively, you can grill mushrooms on a well-seasoned barbecue.) To serve, slice Portobello mushrooms and place on a platter with other mushrooms, sprinkle with parsley, and drizzle with oil and balsamic vinegar.

MAKES 4 SERVINGS.

Roasted Red Bell Peppers

....

This is the one antipasti dish we really look forward to when we visit our family in France. Roasted red bell peppers are included at almost every French dinner table as an appetizer. The bell peppers in France have an incredible sweetness, so we suggest making this dish in the summer when North American bell peppers taste best.

6 large whole red bell peppers

5 cloves garlic, chopped

⅓ cup chopped fresh parsley

Salt to taste

Freshly ground black pepper to taste

½ cup extra virgin olive oil (see note)

Set oven to broil. Place whole peppers on a baking sheet and broil for about 25 minutes, turning peppers occasionally, until they are charred all over. Remove peppers from oven, place in a bowl, and cover with plastic wrap to keep peppers moist until they are cool enough to handle. Peel away skin of each pepper, cut in half lengthwise, discard seeds, and slice lengthwise into 1-in (2½-cm) strips. Return strips to bowl, add garlic, parsley, salt, pepper, and oil. With a spoon, or even better, with your hands, mix until ingredients are well combined. Check for seasoning and serve on a platter.

MAKES 4 SERVINGS.

DO NOT USE ANYTHING LESS THAN QUALITY 100% EXTRA VIRGIN OLIVE OIL FOR THIS DISH. YOU'LL BE GLAD YOU DID!

Fennel à l'Orange

3 fennel bulbs

4 tbsp olive oil

1 tsp salt

½ tsp herbes de Provence
(see note on page 27)

1 tsp garlic, chopped

1 tsp fennel seed

2 cups white wine

1 cup water

3 oranges: zest from
1 orange and freshly
squeezed juice from all 3

For optimum taste and best results, make sure the fennel is cooked enough so a fork can easily pierce it. Serve as an antipasti or to accompany a piece of fish.

Cut each fennel bulb into 8 wedges. Place fennel in a large bowl, add 2 tbsp oil, salt, and herbes de Provence, and toss well. On a barbecue or stovetop grill on high, grill each side of fennel just enough to make grill marks. Set aside. In a frying pan on medium, heat remaining 2 tbsp olive oil. Add garlic and fennel seed and sauté for about 2 minutes, just until garlic is translucent. Deglaze pan with white wine and water. Add zest of 1 orange and pre-grilled fennel. Cook on medium heat for 10 minutes, until fennel is tender, then add juice from 3 oranges and reduce temperature to simmer for another 5 minutes. Remove fennel and place on a platter. Let liquid in pan reduce slightly, then pour over fennel.

Makes 4 servings.

Roasted Chicken with Olives & Garlic Confit

....

This antipasti dish can also be served as a main course alongside roasted potatoes.

Preheat oven to 400°F (205°C). In a large roasting pan, place chicken pieces and coat with herbes de Provence, ¼ cup oil, salt, and pepper. Place garlic in aluminium foil, drizzle with 1 tsp oil, and wrap. Place wrapped garlic alongside chicken in pan and roast for 25 minutes, until chicken pieces are browned and crispy. In a small pot on medium-high heat, bring stock to a full boil, then reduce heat to simmer for about 6 minutes, stirring continually, to reduce liquid and impart more body and flavor. When garlic is cool enough to touch, squeeze the soft, roasted cloves from skins. Add garlic cloves and olives to stock, and stir to combine. Check for seasoning. To serve, place chicken in a serving dish and pour sauce overtop.

MAKES 4 SERVINGS.

ASK YOUR BUTCHER TO CUT THE CHICKEN INTO PIECES WITHOUT REMOVING THE BONES.

WE PURCHASE OUR VEAL STOCK FROM THE STOCK MARKET LOCATED IN THE BUSTLING GRANVILLE ISLAND PUBLIC MARKET IN VANCOUVER. VEAL STOCK IS AVAILABLE FROM YOUR LOCAL GOURMET OR SPECIALTY MARKET.

1 whole fryer chicken (about 3 lb/1⅓ kg), chopped into pieces (see note)

1 tbsp herbes de Provence (see note on page 27)

¼ cup olive oil (for roasting chicken)

Salt to taste

Freshly ground black pepper to taste

2 bulbs garlic, unpeeled

1 tsp olive oil (for roasting garlic)

2 cups veal stock (see note)

½ cup Kalamata olives (pitted if you wish)

MERGUEZ SAUSAGE

I remember when Jean-Francis first introduced me to North African merguez sausage in Marseille. With a large Moroccan and Algerian population in the South of France, the French have incorporated some of their culinary specialities into their own cuisine. Merguez sausage is made with lamb and flavored with Harissa, a spicy red chili pepper paste. Serve warm with baguette. —A.

On a barbecue or under an oven broiler, grill sausages until fully cooked, turning occasionally. Set aside and let cool. In a sauté pan on medium, heat oil. Add onion, fennel, and garlic, and sauté to sweat onions for 2–3 minutes. Deglaze with white wine and Tabasco and Worcestershire sauces. Continue to cook until onions and fennel are soft and transparent. Check for seasoning. Add tomato sauce and reduce heat to simmer for 5 minutes. Cut sausages into bite-sized pieces and add to pan, stirring to combine. Serve, garnished with fresh herbs.

MAKES 8 SERVINGS.

MERGUEZ, OR SPICY LAMB SAUSAGE, IS AVAILABLE AT SPECIALTY BUTCHERS OR MARKETS.

2 lb (900 g) merguez sausage (see note)

¼ cup olive oil

1 medium onion, julienned

1 fennel bulb, julienned

2 tbsp garlic, chopped

¾ cup (180 mL) white wine

1 tbsp Tabasco sauce

1 tbsp Worcestershire sauce

4 cups Tomato Sauce (page 87)

Fresh herbs (e.g. parsley, basil, and chives), chopped (for garnish) (see note)

Appetizers, Soups & Salads

Salade Forestière

Marinated Goat Cheese

Warm Goat Cheese Salad

Mushroom Tartelettes

Fresh Tomato Tarte

Cassolette d'Escargot

Seared Jumbo Squid with Radicchio,
Spinach & Chickpeas

Crabcakes

Antipasto di Mare

Seared Oysters

Oysters Provençal

Fresh Oysters with Pear Mignonette

Oven-Baked Sardines

Cannellini Beans with Sautéed
Calamari

Soupe au Pistou
(Provençal Vegetable Soup)

Soupe aux Moules de Mamie Suzanne

Fish Soup with Crostini

Crostini

Cold Tomato Soup

Salade Forestière

....

Mamie Suzanne (Jean-Francis's mother) created this luxurious salad. She used to serve it in her restaurant, Le Patalain, in Marseille during the fall months. When we worked there, a local farmer would deliver fresh rabbits that we had to skin and gut for this recipe—not something I like to recall, but it was an incredible learning experience! —A.

In a large roasting pan or bowl, combine all ingredients for marinade. Add rabbit loins, and coat with marinade. Cover and refrigerate for 12–24 hours, turning rabbit over halfway through time.

Preheat oven to 350°F (180°C). In a frying pan on high, heat 3 tbsp olive oil. Add mushrooms and sauté for 5 minutes, until browned. Season with 1 tbsp fleur de sel and ¼ tbsp black pepper and set aside. In a separate frying pan on high heat, sear marinated rabbit for 2 minutes on each side, until browned evenly. Transfer rabbit to roasting pan (or if frying pan is oven-proof, just place it in oven) and roast for 7–10 minutes. Remove from oven and let cool. Once cooled, cut into thin slices and set aside. In a bowl, mix all ingredients for vinaigrette until well combined. In a large bowl, toss mixed greens

(continued)

MARINADE:

¼ cup olive oil

½ tsp dried thyme

1 tbsp cognac

1 tsp salt

½ tsp black pepper

2 rabbit loins (see note)

3 tbsp olive oil

1½ cups fresh wild mushrooms (e.g., morels, chanterelles, bluefoots, hedgehogs) (see note)

2 tbsp fleur de sel (see note)

½ tbsp black pepper

VINAIGRETTE:

4 tbsp extra virgin olive oil

3 tbsp balsamic vinegar

Salt to taste

Freshly ground black pepper to taste

3 cups mixed organic greens

¼ cup fresh foie gras (place in freezer for 1 hour to set) (see note)

with vinaigrette. Divide salad among four plates. Separate rabbit slices into four equal portions and place around and over each salad, then add mushrooms. With a potato peeler, shave off five pieces of foie gras per serving and gently place on top of each salad. Sprinkle with remaining 1 tbsp fleur de sel and ¼ tsp black pepper.

MAKES 4 SERVINGS.

RABBIT LOINS CAN BE PURCHASED FROM GOURMET BUTCHERS OR FROM ONLINE SOURCES.

IF YOU CANNOT FIND THESE SPECIFIC FRESH WILD MUSHROOMS, USE MORE COMMON VARIETIES SUCH AS PORTOBELLO, SHIITAKE, AND BUTTON. (DO NOT USE DRIED.)

FLEUR DE SEL IS A HAND-HARVESTED SEA SALT COLLECTED FROM NOIRMOUTIER ISLAND OFF THE COAST OF BRITTANY IN FRANCE. IT IS SLIGHTLY GREY DUE TO THE SANDY MINERALS COLLECTED IN THE PROCESS OF HARVESTING THE TOP LAYER OF SALT BEFORE IT SINKS TO THE BOTTOM OF THE PANS. FLEUR DE SEL CAN BE PURCHASED AT SPECIALTY GROCERS.

FOIE GRAS CAN BE PURCHASED FROM SPECIALTY MARKETS OR GOURMET BUTCHERS.

Marinated Goat Cheese

We love cheese. And as our sons would say, the stinkier the better! Crottin de Chavignol is a milder goat cheese, and when marinated, takes on these beautiful flavors. It's also an impressive display when served with brunch. This recipe requires a sealable jar large enough to fit all the ingredients listed. Serve as an appetizer with a cheese platter, alongside bread and crackers.

6–8 rounds Crottin de Chavignol cheese (see note)

2 sprigs fresh thyme, chopped

1 sprig fresh rosemary

1 sprig fresh marjoram

2–3 garlic cloves, halved

1 tbsp whole black peppercorns, chopped

2 small whole red chili peppers (optional)

2 cups extra virgin olive oil (more or less, depending on size of jar)

In a large jar, arrange cheese, thyme, rosemary, and marjoram. Add garlic, peppercorns, and chili peppers. Fill jar with enough oil to cover ingredients. Close jar tightly with lid and refrigerate for at least 8 days before serving.

MAKES 6–8 MARINATED CHEESE ROUNDS.

CROTTIN DE CHAVIGNOL CHEESE COMES IN A ROUND SHAPE AND IS AVAILABLE FROM SPECIALTY CHEESE SUPPLIERS AND GOURMET GROCERS.

THE MARINATED CHEESE WILL KEEP IN THE REFRIGERATOR FOR UP TO 6 WEEKS.

Warm Goat Cheese Salad

....

This has been our most popular dish since we opened our first restaurant, one which people come from miles away to enjoy. The salad is best served as part of small or intimate dinners, as it gets messy if you cook more than 4 pieces of goat cheese at a time.

TO PREPARE VINAIGRETTE: In a bowl, add mustard, vinegar, salt, and pepper and whisk to combine. Slowly add oil, continuing to whisk until emulsified. Set aside.

TO PREPARE SALAD: Slice goat cheese into 4 round pieces. (A good trick to cleanly slice goat cheese is to use plain dental floss: holding each end of string, place under width of goat cheese log and pull through.) Place goat cheese slices in a bowl, cover with plastic wrap, and refrigerate while preparing salad. In a large bowl, combine breadcrumbs and herbes de Provence. In a separate bowl, beat eggs. In another separate bowl, place flour. Remove goat cheese slices from refrigerator. Dip and coat each cheese slice in flour, then egg, then breadcrumb mixture, then return to bowl and refrigerate for another 10 minutes to firm up. Place 1 cup mixed greens on each plate and evenly distribute vinaigrette over top. In a frying pan on high, heat oil. Sear breaded cheese rounds on each side for about 1 minute until edges just turn golden brown. Place 1 seared cheese slice on side of each salad, and serve.

MAKES 4 SERVINGS.

(continued)

VINAIGRETTE:

1 tsp Dijon mustard

3 tbsp balsamic vinegar

Salt to taste

Freshly ground black pepper to taste

½ cup extra virgin olive oil

SALAD:

10½ oz (300 g) firm ripened goat cheese

2 cups breadcrumbs

1 tbsp herbes de Provence (see note on page 27)

2 eggs

1 cup flour

4 cups mixed greens

3 tbsp olive oil

To garnish the salad plate, try a balsamic reduction also known as *crema di balsamico*. You can purchase it at specialty food shops, or to make on your own: In a saucepan on high, heat 1 cup of inexpensive balsamic vinegar for about 10 minutes, until it reduces to ¼ cup. Let cool before using, then drizzle crema di balsamico around edges of each plate, surrounding salad. Refrigerate leftovers.

MUSHROOM TARTELETTES

This combination of mushrooms and Gorgonzola, the blue-veined cheese from Italy, is heavenly, but if you are not a fan of blue, use a milder cheese such as Brie or Camembert. Serve as an appetizer on its own or on a small bed of mixed greens.

Preheat oven to 375°F (190°C). Line a baking sheet with parchment paper. Place pastry rounds on sheet and pierce with a fork. Bake for 10 minutes, until golden brown. Remove from oven and set aside. Increase oven temperature to 450°F (230°C). In a frying pan on medium-high, heat oil. Add garlic and all mushrooms and sauté for 5 minutes, until mushrooms are soft and all their liquid has evaporated. Add salt and pepper and stir in parsley. Strain excess water if necessary. Remove from heat and allow to cool slightly. Evenly distribute mushrooms on each pastry round and top with cheese. Bake for 3–5 minutes, just until cheese has melted.

MAKES 4 SERVINGS.

PUFF PASTRY, WHICH IS CALLED *PÂTÉ FEUILLETÉE* IN FRANCE, IS SOLD FROZEN IN SHEETS AND IS AVAILABLE IN MOST GROCERY STORES. AFTER THAWING TO USE, KEEP IT COVERED WITH A MOIST TOWEL TO PREVENT IT FROM DRYING.

1 puff pastry sheet, cut into 4-in (10-cm) rounds (see note)

¼ cup extra virgin olive oil

1 tbsp garlic, chopped

1 cup Portobello mushrooms, sliced

1 cup oyster mushrooms, sliced

1 cup button mushrooms, sliced

1 tsp salt

½ tsp black pepper

¼ cup fresh parsley, chopped

½ cup Gorgonzola cheese, crumbled

FRESH TOMATO TARTE

....

**PÂTE BRISÉE
(PASTRY DOUGH):**

1⅔ cups flour

½ tsp salt

6 tbsp cold unsalted
butter, cut into small
pieces

1 egg yolk

3 tbsp ice cold water

2 tbsp Dijon mustard

1 cup Gruyère cheese,
thinly sliced

3 medium red tomatoes,
sliced

2 medium yellow
tomatoes, sliced

½ medium sweet red
onion, sliced

¼ cup Niçoise olives
(may use Kalamata)

1 tbsp extra virgin
olive oil

¼ tsp sea salt

⅛ tsp black pepper

This recipe was inspired by our neighbors in France who invited us over for an aperitif one very beautiful afternoon. Since then, Alessandra often serves this tarte for afternoon lunches or as an appetizer during the summer months when tomatoes are in season. The pâte brisée *is also used in Alessandra's Sunday Quiche (page 171). This recipe requires a 9-in (20-cm) tarte pan which, in contrast to a pie pan, has a removable bottom and straight sides.* —JF.

TO PREPARE PÂTE BRISÉE: In a food processor, add flour, salt, and butter, and pulse until butter resembles small peas. Add egg yolk and continue to pulse to combine. Add ice cold water and pulse again until pastry separates from sides of bowl (may need extra ice cold water if this isn't happening). Remove dough and knead on a lightly floured surface for 1 minute. Form into a ball, cover with plastic wrap, and refrigerate for 1 hour.

Preheat oven to 375°F (190°C). Remove dough from refrigerator and roll to fit a 9-in (20-cm) tarte pan. Brush mustard over dough.

Distribute cheese evenly over mustard. Arrange tomatoes on top of cheese and top with onions and olives. Bake for 30–35 minutes, until crust is golden brown. Serve warm, drizzled with oil and sprinkled with salt and pepper.

MAKES 6 SERVINGS.

PÂTE BRISÉE (MEANING BROKEN-TEXTURED PASTRY) IS A SIMPLE AND DELICIOUS SHORT-CRUST PASTRY SHELL.

IN THE SUMMER MONTHS, TRY THIS RECIPE WITH THE BEAUTIFUL AND DELECTABLE HEIRLOOM TOMATOES, AVAILABLE AT FARMERS' MARKETS.

Cassolette d'Escargot

....

Traditionally, escargots (snails) are drenched in butter and garlic and served in their shells; however, they are quite versatile and can handle many strong flavors. Here, we combine escargots deliciously with mushrooms, olives, and tomato sauce. Serve hot with baguette. Cassolette *means a small individual dish.*

In a large frying pan on high heat, melt butter. Add mushrooms and sauté for about 5 minutes, until brown around edges. Add garlic and escargots and sauté for 3–4 minutes, until mushrooms are soft. Add wine, stirring continually for 2–3 minutes, until liquid is reduced by half. Reduce heat to medium, add tomato sauce, olives, salt, and pepper, and stir to combine. Stir in parsley, chives, and basil, and serve.

Makes 4 servings.

Escargots are commonly sold canned; usually in 2- and 3-dozen portions. Canned escargots have been removed from their shells and cooked in a *court-bouillon* prior to canning; sometimes this cooking broth is included in the can. Drain and rinse snails under running water before use (some recipes may require you to reserve the broth). Canned escargots can be purchased at most specialty and gourmet markets. Escargots in their shells can only be purchased from snail farms.

½ cup butter

2 cups button mushrooms, sliced

1½ tbsp garlic, chopped

36 escargots (see note)

¼ cup white cooking wine

1 cup Tomato Sauce, strained (page 87)

20 Niçoise olives, pitted (if unavailable, use Kalamata)

Salt to taste

Freshly ground black pepper to taste

2 tbsp fresh parsley, chopped

2 tbsp chives, chopped

2 tbsp fresh basil leaves, chopped

SEARED JUMBO SQUID WITH RADICCHIO, SPINACH & CHICKPEAS

2 large squid, cleaned
(see note)

¼ cup olive oil
(for searing squid)

½ tsp salt

1 tbsp black pepper

¼ cup + 2 tbsp extra
virgin olive oil

1 tbsp garlic, chopped

1 cup cooked chickpeas
(garbanzo beans)

6 cups fresh spinach,
chopped

⅓ head of radicchio,
cut or torn into rough
pieces

1 lemon, cut in wedges

Our family loves squid, but we know it's not everyone's favorite! This book offers a few different ways to prepare squid, which we hope will help you to appreciate this delicious and versatile treat from the sea. A refreshing rosé wine would be lovely with this dish.

Preheat oven to 400°F (205°C). Cut squid with a knife and score tubes. In a frying pan on high, heat ¼ cup olive oil. Season squid with salt and pepper and sear for only 1 minute on each side, until slightly golden brown; do not overcook. Transfer squid to a baking pan and place in oven to finish cooking for 2–3 minutes. Meanwhile in a separate pan on medium, heat ¼ cup extra virgin olive oil. Add garlic and chickpeas and sauté for 2–3 minutes. Add spinach and radicchio and cook until spinach is just wilted. Taste test and season with salt and pepper if needed. To serve, place vegetable mixture in middle of platter; remove squid from oven, cut each piece in half again, and place on top of vegetables. Squeeze fresh lemon juice and drizzle remaining extra virgin olive oil over all.

MAKES 4 SERVINGS.

FRESH SQUID CAN BE PURCHASED AT YOUR LOCAL SEAFOOD MARKET. IF FRESH SQUID IS NOT AVAILABLE, YOU MAY SUBSTITUTE WITH FROZEN, WHICH IS AVAILABLE FROM MOST SUPERMARKETS.

CRABCAKES

....

Crabcakes are a North American treat, especially on the West Coast. Here is our version.

In a medium saucepan on high heat, bring water, salt, and potatoes to a boil. Once boiling, reduce heat to medium and cook for 8–10 minutes, until potatoes are soft and a knife can pierce through them easily. Meanwhile, squeeze out and discard all excess liquid from crab and shrimp and set aside. Drain saucepan, and while potatoes are still warm, peel off and discard skins, then place in a bowl and mash. In a mixer, combine egg whites and Worcestershire, Tabasco, and Velouté sauces, and mashed potato and mix until smooth. In a large bowl, combine crab, shrimp, tomatoes, and green onions, and stir until well combined. Add seafood mixture to egg mixture and fold to combine. Fold in 1 cup breadcrumbs. If mixture is too wet, add additional breadcrumbs, 1 tbsp at a time, to desired consistency. Form into 4–5-in (10–13-cm) cakes, packing firmly with hands. Place crabcakes on a tray, cover, and refrigerate for at least 2 hours (see note). When you're ready to serve, remove from refrigerator and lightly coat each cake evenly with flour. In a frying pan on high, heat ¼ cup oil. Sear crabcakes a couple at a time for about 2 minutes to brown, then flip to cook other side for 2 minutes to brown. Repeat for rest of crabcakes, using additional oil if necessary.

MAKES 8 SERVINGS.

THE CRABCAKES CAN ALSO BE KEPT FROZEN FOR UNEXPECTED GUESTS; TO SERVE, THAW, THEN SEAR AS INSTRUCTED.

2 cups water

½ tbsp salt

½ large russet potato, quartered

1 lb (455 g) cooked crab meat

1 lb (455 g) cooked baby shrimp meat

⅓ cup + 1½ tbsp (100 mL) egg whites

1¾ tbsp Worcestershire sauce

1¾ tbsp Tabasco sauce

⅓ cup + 1½ tbsp (100 mL) Velouté Sauce (page 85)

1½ cups tomatoes, diced

¾ cup green onions, minced

½ cup breadcrumbs (or more if necessary)

½ cup flour (for dusting)

2 tbsp oil (or more if necessary)

Antipasto di Mare

1 cup white wine

½ lb (225 g) fresh mussels, cleaned and de-bearded (see note)

½ lb (225 g) fresh clams, cleaned (see note)

8 fresh scallops (see note)

8 fresh prawns, shelled (keep tails on) and deveined (see note)

1 cup Virgin Sauce (page 86)

¼ cup fresh herbs (e.g., parsley, chives, basil), chopped

2 tbsp extra virgin olive oil

Jean-Francis and I discovered this seafood dish while traveling through the Italian Riviera, east of Provence. In the small town of Portofino, we found ourselves lost on a winding cobblestone street. At the end of the path, we discovered a small restaurant called Sailors, but we're not sure why it was called it that because the majority of customers were the local Italian police! We were pleasantly surprised by the quality and freshness of the food. We stayed all afternoon, foregoing the sights, and chatted with the owner. I even got my picture taken with a few of the cute polizia! —A.

In a large pot on high heat, bring wine, mussels, clams, scallops, prawns, and Virgin Sauce to a boil. Once mussels and clams have opened, in about 4 minutes, remove pot from heat. Discard any mussels or clams that have not opened. Add herbs and oil and toss to combine. Serve immediately.

Makes 4 servings

PURCHASE THE FRESHEST MUSSELS AND CLAMS POSSIBLE FROM YOUR LOCAL SEAFOOD MARKET, CHOOSING ONES THAT ARE CLOSED TIGHTLY AND DISCARDING ANY THAT ARE OPEN OR BROKEN. FRESH MUSSELS AND CLAMS MUST BE STORED IN THE REFRIGERATOR AND COOKED THE SAME DAY OF PURCHASE.

WHEN PURCHASING SCALLOPS AND PRAWNS, SELECT ONES THAT ARE LARGE ENOUGH TO BE COUNTED 20–30 SCALLOPS PER KG (OR 10–15 PER LB), AND 16-20 PRAWNS PER KG (OR 8–10 PER LB). FOR THIS RECIPE, DO NOT USE BABY SCALLOPS.

THIS RECIPE CAN BE MADE WITH ANY SHELLFISH OF CHOICE.

SEARED OYSTERS

1 cup breadcrumbs

½ cup freshly mixed
herbs (e.g., chives,
basil, parsley), chopped

½ cup flour

2 eggs

12–16 pre-shucked
small–medium oysters
(see note)

¼ cup olive oil

4 cups mixed greens

3 tbsp Dijon Balsamic
Vinaigrette (page 90)

1 lemon, cut into wedges
(for garnish)

1 pinch fleur de sel
(for garnish) (see note)

Oysters are something that many people do not prepare at home because shucking them can be a challenge. However, for this recipe, we recommend using pre-shucked oysters found at most seafood markets; just ensure you buy the small to medium variety. Oysters are at their best during the winter months when the waters are cold.

In a food processor, add breadcrumbs and herbs and pulse for about 2 minutes, until herbs are well distributed throughout mixture. Transfer to a bowl and set aside. Place flour in a separate bowl and set aside. In another bowl, beat eggs and set aside. Dip each oyster in flour, coating all sides well, then dip into egg mixture until well coated, then dip in breadcrumbs until well coated, then set aside on a plate. Cover and refrigerate for 10 minutes. In a large frying pan on high, heat oil. Sear oysters on each side for about 1 minute, and set aside; this may need to be done in batches. In a large bowl, toss mixed greens with vinaigrette, then divide evenly onto 4 plates. Place 3–4 oysters around each salad and garnish with a lemon wedge for squeezing and a couple flakes of fleur de sel on each oyster.

MAKES 4 SERVINGS.

WE USE FANNY BAY OYSTERS FROM VANCOUVER ISLAND FOR THIS RECIPE. PRE-SHUCKED OYSTERS ARE AVAILABLE AT MOST SEAFOOD MARKETS. SERVE OYSTERS THE SAME DAY OF PURCHASE, KEEPING THEM COOL AT ALL TIMES ON CLEAN ICE OR IN THE REFRIGERATOR.

FLEUR DE SEL IS A HAND-HARVESTED SEA SALT COLLECTED FROM NOIRMOUTIER ISLAND OFF THE COAST OF BRITTANY IN FRANCE. IT IS SLIGHTLY GREY DUE TO THE SANDY MINERALS COLLECTED IN THE PROCESS OF HARVESTING THE TOP LAYER OF SALT BEFORE IT SINKS TO THE BOTTOM OF THE PANS. FLEUR DE SEL CAN BE PURCHASED AT SPECIALTY GROCERS.

OYSTERS PROVENÇAL

....

12–16 pre-shucked
oysters, left in the
half-shell (see note)

1 cup Virgin Sauce
(page 86)

1 tsp fleur de sel
(for garnish) (see note on
page 57)

Our family loves fresh oysters, especially our sons, who can easily devour a couple dozen in one sitting. They like them so much, we thought that if we cooked them they may not eat as many. We were wrong!

Preheat oven to 500°F (260°C). Place oysters shell-side down on baking sheet and top each with 1–1½ tbsp Virgin Sauce. Bake for 5 minutes, until tomatoes from Virgin Sauce just start to brown around edges. Remove from oven, divide onto 4 plates, and serve hot, sprinkled with fleur de sel.

MAKES 4 SERVINGS.

OYSTERS ARE AT THEIR BEST DURING THE WINTER MONTHS WHEN THE WATERS ARE COLD. PRE-SHUCKED OYSTERS ARE AVAILABLE AT MOST SEAFOOD MARKETS. SERVE OYSTERS THE SAME DAY OF PURCHASE, KEEPING THEM COOL AT ALL TIMES ON CLEAN ICE OR IN THE REFRIGERATOR.

FRESH OYSTERS WITH PEAR MIGNONETTE

....

A mignonette *is a traditional French sauce usually made of wine vinegar, shallots, and freshly ground black pepper served with oysters. For this recipe, we wanted to create something a little different, so we used pear vinegar instead and incorporated fresh pears. It's fantastic with any type of fresh oysters.*

In a bowl, mix all mignonette ingredients together until well combined. Serve on the side with fresh shucked oysters.

MAKES ¾ CUP MIGNONETTE; 6—8 SERVINGS.

PEAR VINEGAR IS AVAILABLE AT MOST SPECIALTY MARKETS AND GOURMET GROCERS.

OYSTERS ARE AT THEIR BEST DURING THE WINTER MONTHS WHEN THE WATERS ARE COLD. PRE-SHUCKED OYSTERS ARE AVAILABLE AT MOST SEAFOOD MARKETS. SERVE OYSTERS THE SAME DAY OF PURCHASE, KEEPING THEM COOL AT ALL TIMES ON CLEAN ICE OR IN THE REFRIGERATOR.

MIGNONETTE:

1½ tbsp shallots, minced

1 tbsp black pepper

¾ cup pear vinegar
(see note)

½ small pear, minced
(any type of pear is good)

24 pre-shucked fresh
oysters, left in half-shell
(see note)

Oven-Baked Sardines

3 tbsp olive oil

½ tsp salt

¼ tsp black pepper

12–18 fresh whole sardines, fileted (see note)

1 tbsp extra virgin olive oil (for finishing)

⅛ cup mixed fresh herbs (e.g., basil, chives, parsley), chopped (for garnish)

Fresh sardines are not always easy to find. You may be able to ask your seafood supplier to order them for you. It's well worth it!

Preheat oven to 380°F (195°C). Drizzle oil evenly on a baking pan and season with half the amount of salt and pepper. Place filets flesh-side down, sprinkling with remaining salt and pepper. Bake for 1–2 minutes (no longer; sardines cook very quickly). Remove from oven and serve immediately, drizzled with extra virgin olive oil and garnished with fresh herbs.

Makes 4 servings.

If you are not proficient at fileting fish, ask your supplier to filet them for you.

Cannellini Beans with Sautéed Calamari

....

We discovered this dish in a fresh food open market in Barcelona, Spain, when we approached a little L-shaped bar right in the middle of the market with a hungry crowd sitting and standing all around holding plates of food and champagne glasses. We waited for some seats to be available and then were served several delicious tapas by a wonderful older gentleman who turned out to be the owner, named Pinocchio. Other patrons were ordering food even before they could get a seat, just to get a taste of what the master was dishing out. Fresh squid, escargot, prawns—we thought we had died and gone to heaven! Serve this appy with bread or a side salad.

¾ cup dried cannellini (white kidney) beans (or white navy beans), soaked overnight

2 cups chicken or fish stock (+ additional ¼ cup, if needed)

2 cups fresh squid tubes and tentacles, cleaned (see note)

¼ cup olive oil

Freshly ground black pepper to taste

Salt to taste

¼ cup white wine

1 tsp garlic, chopped

Juice of 1 lemon

½ cup Virgin Sauce (page 86)

Fresh basil (or fresh herb of choice), chopped (for garnish)

In a large pot on high heat, combine beans and stock and bring to a boil. Once boiling, reduce heat to simmer for about 30 minutes, until beans are tender. Separate squid tubes from tentacles with a knife and score or slice squid tubes. In a large pan on high, heat ⅛ cup oil. Add squid, season with salt and pepper, and sear for just 1–2 minutes on each side (do not overcook; they should still be slightly undercooked), then set aside on a plate. Reduce heat to medium-high and deglaze with wine. Add garlic, remaining ⅛ cup olive oil, and lemon juice, and stir to combine. Add beans, and sauté for 3 minutes. If there is not enough liquid, add extra stock if needed, 1 tbsp at a time. Add Virgin Sauce and squid, stir briefly to combine, then immediately remove from heat (to avoid overcooking squid). Transfer to a serving platter, sprinkle with basil, and serve.

MAKES 4 SERVINGS.

FRESH SQUID CAN BE PURCHASED AT YOUR LOCAL FISH MARKET. IF FRESH SQUID IS NOT AVAILABLE, YOU MAY SUBSTITUTE WITH FROZEN, WHICH IS AVAILABLE FROM MOST SUPERMARKETS.

Soupe au Pistou (Provençal Vegetable Soup)

PISTOU:

2 cups fresh basil leaves

4 cloves garlic, minced

1 cup Parmesan cheese, grated

¼ cup extra virgin olive oil

2½ qt (2½ L) water

1 cup canned white coco beans or navy beans, drained and rinsed (see note)

1 cup fresh green beans (or flat broad beans), cut into ¾-in (2-cm) pieces

¾ cup carrots, finely diced

½ cup new potatoes, finely diced

1 cup zucchini, finely diced

1½ tbsp salt

1 tbsp black pepper

1 fresh bouquet garni (see note)

½ cup dry vermicelli noodles (optional)

4 ripe tomatoes, finely diced

This is a delicious vegetarian soup. Pistou *(or "pesto" sauce) is made of garlic, basil, and olive oil, and provides the flavor base for this soup. The ingredients list may look daunting but the actual cooking process is simple. Serve hot with rustic country bread on the side.*

TO PREPARE PISTOU: With a mortar and pestle, add basil, garlic, and cheese to mortar and pound with pestle until ingredients are thoroughly combined and form a smooth purée. (If you do not have a mortar and pestle, this process can also been done using a food processor.) Gradually add oil and pound (or purée) until paste is well blended and smooth.

Fill a large pot with water and place on high heat (see note). Add coco or navy beans, green beans, carrots, potatoes, zucchini, 1 tbsp salt, ¾ tbsp pepper, and bouquet garni, and bring to a boil. Once boiling, reduce heat to medium and cook for 30 minutes, stirring continually. Season with remaining ½ tbsp salt and ¼ tbsp pepper and set aside.

Taste test; it may need more time to cook to bring out flavors of vegetables. Add noodles, and cook for another 10–12 minutes. Add tomatoes, stir to combine, then stir in pistou. Increase heat to return soup to a boil for 3 minutes, then serve.

MAKES 4–5 SERVINGS.

IF USING DRIED COCO OR NAVY BEANS, YOU WILL NEED ONLY ½ CUP TO YIELD 1 CUP COOKED. IN THE POT OF WATER, FIRST BRING DRIED BEANS TO A BOIL, THEN REDUCE HEAT TO SIMMER FOR 15 MINUTES BEFORE ADDING OTHER VEGETABLES.

AVAILABLE AT MOST SPECIALTY MARKETS, A *BOUQUET GARNI* IS A BUNDLE OF FRESH OR DRIED HERBS, USUALLY THYME, BAY LEAVES, AND PARSLEY, TRADITIONALLY USED IN FRANCE TO FLAVOR FRENCH SOUPS. FOR THIS RECIPE, ENSURE THE BOUQUET GARNI IS FRESH AND INCLUDES BAY LEAVES.

Soupe aux Moules de Mamie Suzanne

MUSSELS:

6 lb (2¾ kg) fresh mussels, cleaned and de-bearded (see note)

3 cups + 3 tbsp (750 mL) white wine

1 cup water

1 cup fresh parsley, chopped

1 tbsp fennel seeds (or 1 bunch dried fennel stalks if available)

1 large onion, chopped

SOUP:

3 tbsp butter

3 cloves garlic, chopped

1 large onion, chopped

½ cup fresh parsley, chopped

2 bay leaves

2 tbsp fennel seeds, tied in a small cheesecloth

¼ cup tomato paste

¼ cup flour

½ cup white wine

½ cup water

1½ tsp saffron threads (see note)

Salt to taste

Freshly ground black pepper to taste

This recipe is a labor of love and not inexpensive to make; but the result is sublime. It's a meal in itself that's perfect after a long day outdoors, skiing or hiking. While enjoying this soup, don't forget to close your eyes and imagine you're in the South of France! Serve with some garlic-rubbed croutons and a drizzle of crème fraîche if you wish.

TO PREPARE MUSSELS: In a large stock pot on high heat, steam half the amount of mussels in half the amount of wine, water, parsley, fennel seeds, and onions for 4–5 minutes. After mussels open, remove pot from heat (discard mussels that do not open). With a slotted spoon, transfer opened mussels to a bowl, then strain broth from pot into a container and set aside. Do not discard! With a fork or your hands, remove mussels from shells. Reserve 2 mussels per serving as garnish, then place remaining mussels in a food processor. Purée for 2 minutes then transfer to a bowl. Repeat with remaining mussels, wine, water, parsley, fennel seeds, and onions.

TO PREPARE SOUP: In the same stock pot on medium heat, melt butter. Add garlic, onions, and parsley and sauté for 5 minutes, allowing onions to sweat gently but not change color. Add bay leaves and fennel seeds and stir to combine. Stir in tomato paste and puréed mussels. Sprinkle flour over mixture, stirring continually until flour has been fully absorbed. Add reserved broth, wine, and water. Simmer on medium heat for 15–20 minutes. Add saffron, stir to combine, and simmer for another 10 minutes. Season with salt and pepper, garnish each serving with 2 reserved mussels, and serve.

MAKES 10 SERVINGS (SEE NOTE).

PURCHASE THE FRESHEST MUSSELS POSSIBLE FROM YOUR LOCAL SEAFOOD MARKET, CHOOSING ONES THAT ARE CLOSED TIGHTLY AND DISCARDING ANY THAT ARE OPEN OR BROKEN. FRESH MUSSELS MUST BE STORED IN THE REFRIGERATOR AND COOKED THE SAME DAY OF PURCHASE.

SAFFRON IS THE WORLD'S MOST EXPENSIVE SPICE BY WEIGHT, BUT A LITTLE GOES A LONG WAY. DERIVED FROM THE FLOWER OF THE SAFFRON CROCUS, IT TAKES 75,000 BLOSSOMS TO MAKE A SINGLE POUND OF SAFFRON THREADS.

THIS RECIPE YIELDS 10 SERVINGS, BUT GIVEN THE TIME AND COST, IT'S NOT WORTH REDUCING THE RECIPE TO SERVE LESS PEOPLE. IT CAN BE MADE 1 DAY IN ADVANCE, AND STORED IN THE REFRIGERATOR UNTIL READY TO BE REHEATED.

Fish Soup with Crostini

....

This recipe requires time and attention to make, but this wouldn't be a book about Provençal cooking without a fish soup recipe. We serve it as a starter; it is also used as the stock for the Bouillabaisse (page 115). Cooked properly, the aroma of this soup will be reminiscent of the Mediterranean Sea. For this recipe, you will need at large stock pot that has at least a 2½-gal (10 L) volume.

In a large frying pan on high, heat 3 tbsp oil. Add ¼ of the amount of red snapper and fish scraps and sear for 5–8 minutes on each side, until browned, then place in a large stock pot. Repeat until all fish has been seared. Reduce heat of frying pan to medium-high, add fennel, onions, and garlic and sauté for about 5 minutes, until golden brown. Add tomato paste, stir, and continue to sauté for another 2 minutes. Add vegetable mixture to stock pot, along with water, salt, and saffron, and increase heat to bring to a boil. Once boiling, reduce heat to simmer for about 2½ hours, until fish is falling off bones and almost melted into soup.

Once soup is cooked, ladle about 4 cups soup into a food processor and purée to thicken (be careful when processing hot liquids). Pour through a sieve into a pot, pressing as much pulp and liquid through sieve as possible. Repeat until all soup is puréed and strained; it

(continued)

1 cup olive oil

5 lb (2¼ kg) red snapper, cut into 2-in (5-cm) steaks

3½ lb (1½ kg) white fish scraps (including bones)

1 fennel bulb, sliced

1 large onion, sliced

1 cup whole garlic cloves

1 can (13½-oz/398-mL) tomato paste

2½ gal (10 L) water

4 tbsp salt

2 tsp saffron threads

1 batch freshly made Crostini (see note)

½ cup Gruyère cheese, grated (for garnish)

Rouille (for garnish) (see note)

should be a burnt orange color. Taste test, as it may need salt. (At this point, make rouille if not yet prepared; see note.) Return pot of strained soup to stovetop to reheat for serving. Serve, with crostini topped with cheese and a dollop of rouille.

MAKES 15 SERVINGS.

SEE OPPOSITE PAGE FOR CROSTINI RECIPE; PREPARE 10 MINUTES BEFORE SERVING.

SEE PAGE 82 FOR ROUILLE RECIPE, WHICH REQUIRES THIS FISH SOUP AS A BASE. IF YOU DO NOT HAVE ROUILLE PREVIOUSLY PREPARED, MAKE IT ONCE YOU HAVE STRAINED THE SOUP, THEN REHEAT SOUP AND SERVE.

FISH SOUP LEFTOVERS CAN BE STORED IN THE FREEZER FOR UP TO 2 MONTHS.

CROSTINI

....

Crostini, or "little toasts" in Italian, are thin slices of baguette drizzled with olive oil and served warm. They are best topped with finely diced or sliced savory cheeses, vegetables, meat, or seafood, or served with soups. The Bouillabaisse (page 115), Fish Soup (page 67), Fennel & Oven-Dried Tomato Compote (page 80), Tapenade (page 73), Caramelized Fennel & Anchovy Spread (page 76), Chickpea Spread (page 77), and Artichoke Tapenade (page 74) can be served with crostini.

1 baguette, sliced ¼-in (5-mm) thick

2 tbsp olive oil

Preheat oven to 375°F (190°C). On a baking sheet, place baguette slices and brush each with oil. Bake for 7–10 minutes, until golden brown. Remove from oven and let cool.

MAKES 1 BAGUETTE OF CROSTINI.

COLD TOMATO SOUP

....

1 can (17-oz/510-mL) crushed plum tomatoes, strained

1 red bell pepper, finely diced

1 yellow bell pepper, finely diced

4 tomatoes, finely diced

½ tbsp garlic purée

¼ medium sweet red onion, finely diced

1 cucumber, finely diced

6 tbsp + 2 tsp (100 mL) balsamic vinegar

¾ cup + 2½ tbsp (200 mL) extra virgin olive oil

1 tbsp + 1 tsp salt

1½ tbsp Tabasco sauce

1½ tbsp Worcestershire sauce

This recipe is similar to the Spanish and Portuguese cold soup gazpacho; you can make it more substantial (and elegant) with a garnish of fresh crab meat on top of each serving.

In a large bowl, combine all ingredients. Cover and refrigerate overnight to allow flavors to meld together. Before serving, stir to combine, then serve chilled.

MAKES 4 SERVINGS.

Spreads, Sauces & Dressings

Tapenade

Artichoke Tapenade

Anchoïade (Anchovy Dip)

Caramelized Fennel & Anchovy
Spread

Chickpea Spread

Moroccan Salsa

Fennel & Oven-Dried Tomato
Compote

Roasted Red Pepper Aïoli

Rouille

Cumin Cilantro Yogurt

Hollandaise Sauce

Velouté Sauce

Virgin Sauce

Tomato Sauce

Caponata

Cilantro Pesto

Dijon Balsamic Vinaigrette

L'Ancienne Mustard & Lemon
Vinaigrette

TAPENADE

....

When we opened our first restaurant, we wanted to create an atmosphere similar to that of our home, which includes being able to serve something to guests as soon as they arrive. Tapenade is a Provençal spread of olives, capers, and anchovies. It is a perfect hors d'œuvre or snack that can be made in advance and served soon after guests arrive to awaken their tastebuds in preparation for the great meal that awaits them. Serve on Crostini (page 69).

1 cup Niçoise olives, pitted (may substitute with Kalamata)

2½ tbsp capers

1½ tbsp garlic, chopped (about 2 large cloves)

6 anchovy filets

3 tbsp extra virgin olive oil

In a food processor, combine all ingredients and purée until smooth. Serve, and store leftovers in refrigerator for up to 2 weeks.

MAKES ABOUT 1 CUP.

THIS RECIPE CALLS FOR FRENCH NIÇOISE OLIVES, WHICH ARE SMALL AND BROWN OR PURPLISH-BLACK IN COLOR. THEY IMPART A DISTINCT SOUR TASTE; NOT SURPRISINGLY, THEY ARE OFTEN USED IN THE TRADITIONAL NIÇOISE SALAD (NAMED FOR THE REGION OF NICE, FRANCE).

ARTICHOKE TAPENADE

1 can (13½-oz/398-mL)
artichoke hearts, drained

2½ tbsp capers

1½ tbsp garlic, chopped
(about 2 large cloves)

3 tbsp extra virgin
olive oil

6 anchovy filets

A lovely substitute for the traditional Tapenade (page 73) that is made with Niçoise olives, this version is lighter in flavor. Serve with Crostini (page 69).

In a food processor or blender, combine all ingredients and purée until smooth. Serve, and store leftovers in refrigerator for up to 1 week.

MAKES ABOUT 1 CUP.

Anchoïade (Anchovy Dip)

....

Celery is commonly served with this very savory dip, but you can also use the inner leaves of Romaine lettuce, Belgium endive, small cauliflower florets, green onions, fennel slices, radishes, zucchini sticks, baby artichokes (fresh or canned), and cherry tomatoes. This anchoïade *tastes best as an appetizer, served outdoors in summer … don't forget some fresh French bread!*

In a food processor or blender, combine all ingredients except oil and purée until smooth. Slowly add oil while continuing to blend until emulsified. Some traditions in Provence call for this dip to be heated, but this is optional. If desired, transfer to a small pot on medium-low heat to gently warm, then serve. Refrigerate leftovers for up to 1 week.

Makes 4 servings (about 1½ cups).

In this recipe, we use a food processor to blend the ingredients; however, ideally this dip is best made with a mortar and pestle.

Large pinch coarse sea salt

Freshly ground black pepper to taste

Large pinch fresh savory (if unavailable, use fresh parsley or herbes de Provence)

4 garlic cloves, lightly crushed and peeled

20 anchovy filets

1 tsp red wine vinegar

1½ cups extra virgin olive oil

CARAMELIZED FENNEL & ANCHOVY SPREAD

....

¼ cup extra virgin
olive oil

2 fennel bulbs, diced

½ medium onion, diced

2 cloves garlic, minced

1 tsp salt

Water (to deglaze pan)
(optional)

2 anchovy fillets, diced

Anchovies have always received a bad rap, but chefs use them to enhance many types of recipes. In this spread, anchovies are one of two main ingredients. The sweetness of the fennel nicely balances the anchovies' saltiness. Excite your palate with this recipe as a vegetable dip or as a spread on Crostini (page 69).

In a large frying pan on medium, heat oil. Add fennel and onions and slowly sauté for about 6 minutes, until onions are caramelized. Add garlic and salt and cook for another 7 to 10 minutes, stirring occasionally. If pan gets too dry, deglaze with 1–2 tbsp water at a time. Once fennel is tender and has a caramel color, remove pan from heat to let cool. Fold anchovies into cooled fennel mixture and combine well. Transfer to a serving bowl and serve. Store leftovers in refrigerator for up to 5 days.

MAKES ABOUT ¾ CUP.

Chickpea Spread

....

This recipe's roasted, chunky texture makes it very different from hummus. We use this in the restaurant on Crostini (page 69) to spice up a mixed greens salad, or to serve with afternoon tea as a crudité (raw vegetable) dip.

In a sauté pan on medium high, heat oil. Add chickpeas, onion, salt, and pepper and sauté for 4–5 minutes, until chickpeas are a light golden color, onions are soft, and most oil has been absorbed. Add lemon zest and juice, stir to combine, then remove from heat. Transfer to a bowl and use a fork to mash until smooth but retaining some chunky consistency. Serve, drizzled with 1 tbsp extra virgin olive oil, and store leftovers in refrigerator for up to 5 days.

Makes 1 cup.

¼ cup olive oil (for sautéing)

1 can (13½-oz/398-mL) chickpeas (garbanzo beans)

¼ medium sweet red onion, diced

1 tsp salt

½ tsp black pepper

Zest of 1 lemon (zest lemon before juicing, see below)

Juice of 1 lemon

1 tbsp extra virgin olive oil (for finishing)

Moroccan Salsa

....

This salsa's combination of sweet and sour brings out some interesting flavors that complement most fish dishes; try it served on fresh, seared mahi mahi (as shown on opposite page). It can also be used as a topping on crackers.

In a bowl, combine all ingredients and mix with a spoon. Season with salt and pepper and serve. Refrigerate leftovers for up to 3 days.

MAKES ABOUT 2 CUPS.

½ red bell pepper, cut in diamond shapes

½ yellow bell pepper, cut in diamond shapes

¼ small red onion, minced

¼ cup golden raisins

3 tbsp Kalamata olives, chopped

⅛ cup fresh cilantro, chopped

⅛ cup fresh mint, chopped

Juice of ½ lemon

½ tsp orange zest

½ tsp cumin

½ tsp cinnamon

1 pinch cayenne pepper

¼ cup olive oil

Salt to taste

Freshly ground black pepper to taste

Fennel & Oven-Dried Tomato Compote

....

2 cups cherry tomatoes, halved

1 tsp salt

½ tsp black pepper

1 tsp herbes de Provence (see note on page 27)

¾ cup extra virgin olive oil

4 tsp olive oil (for grilling and sautéing fennel)

1 tbsp garlic, chopped

2 fennel bulbs, stalks removed, cored, and cut in wedges ½-in (1-cm) thick

¼ cup fresh parsley, chopped (for garnish)

1 batch Crostini (page 69)

Another tasty spread to serve your guests soon after they arrive. We often put a few bowls of different spreads out on the table to add flavor and color. The tomatoes are oven-dried first to bring out their sweetness.

Preheat oven to 250° F (120°C). On a baking sheet or pan, place tomatoes cut-side up, sprinkle with ½ tsp salt, pepper, and herbes de Provence, and drizzle with ¼ cup extra virgin olive oil. Place in oven (with no fan on) to dry for 1½ hours.

Preheat barbecue or stovetop grill to high. Place fennel in a bowl and season with remaining ½ tsp salt and 2 tsp olive oil. Place fennel directly on grill briefly just to mark each side. Remove from grill, let cool slightly, and dice. In a frying pan on low, heat remaining 2 tsp olive oil and sauté fennel and garlic for 8–10 minutes until completely cooked and soft. In a large bowl, combine sautéed fennel and garlic and tomato mixture and toss with remaining ½ cup oil. Check for seasoning. Garnish with parsley, and serve alongside crostini.

Makes about 1 cup, enough for 1 baguette of crostini.

Roasted Red Pepper Aïoli

....

Aïoli is generally known as a garlic mayonnaise. We've added a twist with roasted red peppers to create a tasty dip for to French fries, crudités, and Crabcakes (page 53).

In a blender or food processor, combine egg yolks, mustard, and garlic and blend until smooth. Add salt and then slowly add oil while continuing to blend until emulsified. Transfer to a large bowl, scraping out all contents from processor. In same blender or processor, purée peppers until smooth, then add to aïoli and whisk together until smooth. Stir in lemon juice and serve. Store leftovers in refrigerator for up to 4 days.

MAKES 3 CUPS.

2 egg yolks

1 tbsp Dijon mustard

1½ tbsp garlic, chopped

½ cup Roasted Red Bell Peppers (page 33), chopped

2 cups canola oil

½ tsp salt

1 tbsp freshly squeezed lemon juice

ROUILLE

2 cups Fish Soup
(page 67)

⅛ tsp saffron threads

1 pinch chili flakes

2 egg yolks

1 tbsp Dijon mustard

1½ tbsp garlic, puréed

2 cups canola oil

¼ tsp salt

A traditional accompaniment to Fish Soup with Crostini (page 67) or Bouillabaisse (page 115), this mayonnaise is subtly spiced with chilies, saffron, and garlic. When served with soup, spread a little rouille on a crostini, top with grated Gruyère cheese, then let it melt in your mouth.

In a saucepan on medium-low heat, combine fish soup, saffron, and chili flakes and let reduce for 25–35 minutes, stirring continually, until about ⅓ cup liquid remains. Remove from heat to cool completely. Meanwhile, in a food processor or blender, combine egg yolks, mustard, and garlic and blend until well combined. Slowly add oil while continuing to blend until emulsified. Transfer to a bowl, add cooled fish soup reduction, and stir to combine. Refrigerate until ready to serve. Store leftovers in refrigerator for up to 3 days.

MAKES ABOUT 3 CUPS.

Cumin Cilantro Yogurt

....

We created this recipe specifically for our Crabcakes. It is a tantalizing lighter alternative to red pepper aïoli. Serve on the side with Crabcakes (page 53) or a vegetable platter.

In a large bowl, combine all ingredients and whisk until well combined. Serve, and store leftovers in refrigerator for up to 3 days; do not freeze.

Makes 2 cups.

2 cups plain yogurt

½ tbsp toasted cumin seeds

¼ cup extra virgin olive oil

½ cup Cilantro Pesto (page 89)

1 tsp salt

HOLLANDAISE SAUCE

2 egg yolks

5 tbsp white wine

4 drops Tabasco sauce

4 drops Worcestershire
sauce

½ lemon

Salt to taste

Freshly ground black
pepper to taste

1 cup clarified butter
(page 182)

This traditional French sauce, which uses eggs as the emulsifying agent, is served on the eggs Benedict recipes (pages 165–167). Hollandaise always tastes best when made from scratch, using clarified butter.

In a large stainless steel bowl, mix all ingredients except clarified butter until well combined. Over a large pot of simmering water (or using a double boiler), place bowl and whisk until mixture becomes thick and fluffy and eggs are cooked through. Remove from heat and slowly whisk in clarified butter, continuing to whisk until emulsified. Taste test and season if desired. Serve immediately.

MAKES ABOUT 2 CUPS.

VELOUTÉ SAUCE

....

Velouté is one of five "Mother Sauces" from which almost all the classic French sauces are derived. It is a base blond sauce that can be flavored many ways. We use it in our Chicken Crêpes (page 172) to add creaminess to the chicken and asparagus. When incorporating Cheddar cheese to a velouté, it becomes a classic sauce for Mac 'n' Cheese! It is also used in the Crabcakes recipe (page 53) to bind the ingredients, or can be used as a base for vegetable gratin topping.

½ cup butter

¼ medium onion, diced

½ cup flour

4 cups chicken stock

½ cup + 2 tsp whipping cream

In a saucepan on medium heat, melt butter. Add onions and sauté for 3 minutes, until onions are translucent. Gradually sprinkle in flour, stirring continually until flour is incorporated. Slowly whisk in 1 cup chicken stock, stirring continually until smooth. Stir in remaining chicken stock, stirring continually again until sauce thickens and comes to a boil. Once boiling, reduce heat to low and stir in whipping cream until smooth. Allow sauce to come to a gentle simmer, then remove from heat. Serve, and store leftovers in refrigerator for up to 5 days.

MAKES 5 CUPS.

Virgin Sauce

....

4 medium tomatoes, diced small

5 fresh basil leaves, julienned

2 cloves garlic, minced

Juice of 1 lemon

4 tbsp extra virgin olive oil

Salt to taste

Freshly ground black pepper to taste

This sauce was Jean-Francis's gift to the Canadian West Coast. When he first arrived in Vancouver, he wanted to create a sauce that was representative of Provence. It contains all the "virgin" ingredients of the South of France, with extra virgin olive oil to bring out a delicious flavor. This light, fresh sauce is versatile, complementing any grilled fish or chicken dish. It can also be tossed in pasta or savored simply on a cracker for bruschetta. —A.

In a bowl, mix all ingredients until well combined. Season with salt and pepper serve. Store leftovers in refrigerator for up to 3 days.

Makes about 1½ cups.

TOMATO SAUCE

....

French or not, a good, basic tomato sauce is something all cooks need to master. It took us a few tries to develop this sauce for our pasta dishes at the restaurant. It's light, very tasty, and simple to make for pasta dishes at home. Refer to the index to find all the recipes that use this sauce.

In a large pan on medium, heat oil. Add onions and sauté for about 2 minutes until just translucent. Add garlic and sauté for another 30 seconds, until garlic has softened slightly. Add tomatoes and its juices, stir, and increase heat to bring to a boil. Once boiling, add salt and oregano, reduce heat to medium-low, and cook for 20–30 minutes, until tomatoes are very soft. Remove from heat and use a hand blender to purée until fairly smooth but retaining some chunks of tomato (alternatively, transfer sauce to a traditional blender to purée; be careful when blending hot liquids). Use immediately, and store leftovers in sealable 2-cup containers in freezer for up to 3 months.

MAKES 6 1/3 CUPS (1½ L).

¼ cup olive oil

1 large onion, diced

1 tbsp garlic, minced

1 can (100-oz/3-L) plum tomatoes (including juices)

2 tbsp salt

1 tbsp dried oregano

CAPONATA

½ cup olive oil

1 eggplant, cut in
½-in (1-cm) cubes

1 red bell pepper,
diced medium

1 cup celery, diced

1 large onion, chopped

1 cup Tomato Sauce
(page 87)

1 pinch sugar

¼ cup red wine vinegar

2 tbsp capers, drained

½ tsp salt

½ tsp black pepper

1 cup black olives,
pitted and chopped

Caponata is a Sicilian sauce featuring tomatoes and eggplant. In our recipe, we have added a Provençal touch, adding olives and vegetables. This is a great sauce for pasta, and it can also accompany grilled chicken breasts.

In a large frying pan on medium-high, heat ¼ cup oil. Add eggplant and sauté until tender and golden brown. Remove eggplant and set aside. In the same pan on medium-high, heat remaining ¼ cup oil and sauté onions, bell pepper, and celery until tender, 5 minutes. Add sautéed eggplant, stir in tomato sauce, and allow mixture to come to a boil, stirring occasionally. Once boiling, cover, and reduce heat to simmer for 5 minutes. Add sugar, vinegar, capers, salt, pepper, and olives and stir to combine. Simmer for another 15 minutes, stirring occasionally. Let cool completely, then refrigerate overnight, as it's always better the next day! To serve, reheat on medium-high, stirring until sauce comes to a boil, then pour over cooked pasta and toss.

MAKES ENOUGH SAUCE FOR 2 SERVINGS OF PASTA.

Cilantro Pesto

....

Cilantro is not a typical Provençal herb; however, it is popular in North American cuisine and is also becoming more common in France. Here, we have taken a traditional Italian pesto (which uses basil) to create a delightful, refreshing sauce that is used in the Cumin Cilantro Yogurt (page 83), or added to chicken soup!

4 cups fresh cilantro leaves

¾ cup pine nuts

¾ cup olive oil

2 tbsp garlic, chopped

Juice of ½ lemon

1 tsp salt

In a food processor or blender, combine all ingredients and purée until smooth. Serve, and store leftovers in refrigerator for up to 1 week.

MAKES 2 CUPS.

SEE THE ROASTED VEGETABLES TOSSED IN PESTO RECIPE ON PAGE 31 FOR A TRADTIONAL VERSION OF PESTO.

Dijon Balsamic Vinaigrette

3 tbsp Dijon mustard

½ cup balsamic vinegar

1 cup extra virgin olive oil

Salt to taste

Freshly ground black pepper to taste

A classic, rustic vinaigrette that is light, tasty, and delicious on any salad.

In a tall container (e.g., a 4-cup/1-L measuring cup), combine mustard and vinegar. With a hand blender, mix until well combined, then slowly add oil, continuing to blend until emulsified. Taste test, season with salt and pepper, and serve. Refrigerate leftovers for up to 2 weeks.

Makes 1½ cups.

L'Ancienne Mustard & Lemon Vinaigrette

This is a basic vinaigrette that is great on any salad, or even as a dip for crudités (raw vegetables). We use it in the restaurant for our seafood salad.

In a bowl, combine mustard, lemon juice, and Tabasco and Worcestershire sauces and whisk until well combined. Slowly stir in honey and oil, then continue to whisk until emulsified. Season with salt and pepper and serve. Store leftovers in refrigerator for up to 1 week.

MAKES ABOUT 1 CUP.

MUSTARDS THAT ARE *L'ANCIENNE*, MEANING "OLD-FASHIONED," ARE GRAINY MUSTARDS BECAUSE TRADITIONALLY, MUSTARDS ARE WHOLE GRAIN, NOT SMOOTH LIKE TODAY.

3 tbsp L'Ancienne mustard

Juice of 1 lemon

Dash of Tabasco sauce

Dash of Worcestershire sauce

1 tbsp honey

⅔ cup extra virgin olive oil

Salt to taste

Freshly ground pepper to taste

Vegetable Mains & Sides

Roasted Vegetable Tartelettes with
Sun-Dried Tomatoes

Chanterelles à la Provençal

Tomatoes Provençal

Grilled Asparagus with Sun-Dried
Tomato Vinaigrette

Curried Baby Eggplant

Artichoke, Peas & Pancetta in Phyllo

Roasted Sweet Potatoes

Seven-Grain Rice with Chickpeas
& Romano Beans

Mushroom & Pearl Barley Risotto
with Truffle Oil

New World Panisse

Soft Parmesan Polenta

Nonna's Manicotti

Orecchiette Pasta with Rapini
& Olives

Warm Potato Salad with L'Ancienne
Mustard Vinaigrette

Roasted Vegetable Tartelettes with Sun-Dried Tomatoes

....

This recipe is most delicious when using fresh organic vegetables. Serve year-round as an appetizer or side dish.

Preheat oven to 375°F (190°C). Line a baking sheet with parchment paper. Place puff pastry rounds on sheet and poke pastry with a fork. Bake for about 10 minutes, until golden brown. Remove from oven and set aside.

Increase oven temperature to 425°F (220°C). Ideally, each vegetable should be roasted separately, but if you have limited oven space and/or pans, you can roast some of them together—for example, bell peppers; carrots, onion, and garlic; eggplant and mushrooms; and, zucchini, which should be roasted separately or added last, as it cooks the fastest. Place vegetables, except sun-dried tomatoes, in roasting pans, season with salt and pepper, and drizzle with ½ cup oil. Roast for 12–15 minutes, except zucchini which requires 8–10 minutes, turning occasionally, until vegetables are softened and browned. Remove from oven and transfer vegetables to a large bowl. Add sun-dried tomatoes and toss to mix. With a small spoon, evenly distribute mixture onto cooked puff pastry rounds, garnish with basil, and drizzle with oil.

Makes 6 tartelettes.

Puff pastry, which is called *pâté feuilletée* in France, is sold frozen in sheets and is available in most grocery stores. After thawing to use, keep it covered with a moist towel to prevent it from drying.

1 sheet puff pastry, cut into 6 (4-in/10-cm) rounds (see note)

¼ red bell pepper, chopped

¼ yellow bell pepper, chopped

1 medium carrot, chopped

½ medium Spanish onion, chopped

½ bulb garlic, peeled

½ medium-large eggplant, chopped

½ cup button mushrooms, quartered

½ medium zucchini, chopped

1 tsp salt

1 tsp black pepper

½ cup olive oil

8 pieces oil-packed sun-dried tomatoes (if using dried, reconstitute in hot water), chopped

4–5 fresh basil leaves, chopped (for garnish)

2 tbsp extra virgin olive oil (for finishing)

Chanterelles à la Provençal

....

2 tbsp butter

2 tbsp extra virgin olive oil

6 cloves garlic, chopped

3½–4 cups fresh chanterelle mushrooms (see note)

Salt to taste

Freshly ground black pepper to taste

¼ cup cognac (optional)

½ cup fresh parsley, chopped

You can make just about anything à la Provençal with a little garlic, parsley, butter, and cognac! Chanterelles complete this quintessential Provençal experience.

In a large pan on medium-high, heat butter, oil, and garlic. Add chanterelles, season with salt and pepper, and sauté for 8–12 minutes until soft. If using cognac, remove pan from heat before carefully adding, then return to heat, letting it flame up (tipping pan towards flame or with a lit match, if necessary) then allowing alcohol to burn off. Add parsley, toss to combine, and serve.

Makes 4 servings.

Chanterelles are wild mushrooms that range in color from orange to bright yellow; native to Europe, they are also found in parts of the Pacific Northwest and along the US east coast. Fresh chanterelles can be found at specialty or gourmet markets.

These mushrooms usually need a thorough cleaning: In a large bowl or sink filled with water, place mushrooms to soak, loosening dirt. Check each mushroom and remove remaining dirt with a cloth or paper towel, then place on another cloth or paper towel to dry. Do not use dried chanterelles for this recipe; they are better used in sauces or stuffing.

Tomatoes Provençal

....

This is another one of those recipes that Mamie Suzanne cooks for us the minute she gets off the plane from France—she knows it's my favorite. The sugar helps to create a deep red, syrupy caramel that is sublime when combined with the garlic and herbs. It's wonderful during summer, when fresh tomatoes are at their peak. Serve with any fish or meat entrée. —A.

In a blender or food processor, add garlic, parsley, ¼ cup oil, salt, pepper, and breadcrumbs (if using) and purée until well combined. In a frying pan on high, heat remaining ¼ cup oil. Place tomatoes cut-side side down and sear for about 1–2 minutes until browned. Reduce heat to low, turn tomatoes over, sprinkle sugar on and around them, and cook for 12–15 minutes. Generously add topping over tomatoes and cook uncovered for another 10 minutes (or bake at 350°F/180°C for 35 minutes), until tomatoes are caramelized and topping is slightly brown.

Makes 4 servings.

3 tbsp garlic, chopped

¾ cup fresh parsley, chopped

½ cup olive oil

1 tsp salt

½ tsp black pepper

¼ cup breadcrumbs (optional)

4 vine-ripened tomatoes, halved

2 tbsp white or brown sugar

Grilled Asparagus with Sun-Dried Tomato Vinaigrette

....

Asparagus is an ideal vegetable to cook on the grill in the summer. It's easy and quick to make and very tasty. Of course, you can also prepare these in a pan on a stovetop, but they won't char as they will on the barbecue. For this recipe, use larger asparagus, which are easier to cook on the grill.

In a bowl, add all vinaigrette ingredients and mix until well combined. Preheat barbecue to high. In a large bowl or dish, combine asparagus and oil, season with salt and pepper, and toss to coat (do not coat in too much oil, or asparagus will flare up on grill). Place asparagus directly on barbecue (ensuring they do not fall through grate) and grill for 2 minutes on each side. Place on a serving platter, drizzle with vinaigrette, and serve.

Makes 4–6 servings.

Asparagus naturally break off at the point where the stems turn woody and hard, so it is easy to snap off this part of the stem.

VINAIGRETTE:

12 pieces oil-packed sun-dried tomatoes (if using dried, reconstitute in hot water), diced

1 tsp garlic, chopped

¼ cup extra virgin olive oil

1 tbsp red wine vinegar

Dash salt

Dash freshly ground black pepper

2 bunches fresh asparagus (about 1 lb/900g), hard stems removed (see note)

1 tbsp olive oil

Dash salt

Dash freshly ground black pepper

CURRIED BABY EGGPLANT

....

¼ cup olive oil

1 tbsp salt

12 baby eggplants, halved lengthwise and flesh scored (see note)

1 tbsp curry powder

½ tsp ground fennel seeds

½ tsp ground coriander seeds

We love eggplant, but we also know that not everyone does. We tell the unconverted that no matter which type of eggplant they are using, it should be cooked thoroughly; when only partially cooked, it can have a bitter taste. The beauty of eggplant is that it acts like a sponge, easily absorbing the flavors of other ingredients. Serve with any lamb dish (pages 156–160) or as an antipasti.

Preheat oven to 375°F (190°C). In a frying pan on medium-high, heat oil. Sprinkle salt on eggplant flesh and place flesh-side down in pan to sear for about 2 minutes, until golden brown and a crust forms along edges. Transfer eggplant to a baking pan, flesh-side up. In a bowl, mix curry powder, fennel seeds, and coriander seeds, then sprinkle over seared eggplant. Cover with aluminium foil and bake for 15–20 minutes, until eggplant is soft to the touch.

MAKES 4 SERVINGS.

BABY EGGPLANT IS SIMPLY SMALLER-SIZED REGULAR EGGPLANT (JAPANESE EGGPLANT IS THE LONGER AND THINNER VARIETY). WHEN PURCHASING, BUY ONES THAT ARE FIRM WITH NO WRINKLES. IF BABY EGGPLANT IS UNAVAILABLE, YOU MAY USE REGULAR EGGPLANT, SLICED, FOR THIS RECIPE.

Artichoke, Peas & Pancetta in Phyllo

....

These baked phyllo pastry packages include a bit of pancetta, *Italian bacon, but otherwise are vegetarian. Instead of phyllo, you could use puff pastry and the same technique on page 95 (Roasted Vegetable Tartelettes) to make the pastry base; alternatively, place the mixture on grilled rustic Italian bread, then bake. Serve this as a light lunch with mixed greens.*

Preheat oven to 375°F (190°C). In a frying pan on high heat, add pancetta and sauté for about 5 minutes. Add onions and garlic and sauté for 2 minutes, until onions are soft. Add artichokes and peas and sauté for 3 minutes, until peas are cooked through. Transfer mixture to a large bowl and let cool to room temperature. Add cheese, pepper, and basil, and mix well to evenly distribute. On a large flat surface, take 1 phyllo sheet and brush entire top side with melted butter. Lay second phyllo sheet on top and again brush entirely with melted butter. Lay third sheet on top and repeat with melted butter. Lay fourth sheet on top, then spread artichoke and pea mixture lengthwise down center. Fold pastry over mixture so it completely encases it as filling. Fold ends under, then brush more melted butter over top of pastry. Line a baking sheet with parchment paper. Place pastry on sheet and bake for 15–20 minutes, until golden brown. To serve, slice into 6 portions.

Makes 6 servings.

½ cup pancetta, diced

½ medium onion, diced

2 cloves garlic, minced

2 cans (13½-oz/398-mL each) artichokes, drained and sliced

1 cup fresh or frozen peas

½ cup Asiago cheese, grated

½ tsp black pepper

6 fresh basil leaves, torn

4 phyllo pastry sheets

½ cup butter, melted

Roasted Sweet Potatoes

....

Our boys love the dark-skinned, orange-fleshed variety of sweet potatoes, which are often referred to as yams (see note). In this recipe, they just melt in your mouth, and Remi and Matisse always fight over who gets the roasted garlic, which becomes sweet and caramelized. Serve with Grilled Quail with Juniper Berry Jus (page 149).

3 medium orange-fleshed sweet potatoes, peeled, each cut into 6 wedges (see note)

7 cloves garlic, unpeeled

4 shallots, halved

¼ cup olive oil

2 tbsp butter, room temperature

1 tsp salt

½ tsp black pepper

Preheat oven to 400°F (205°C). In a bowl, combine all ingredients and toss until well coated with oil. Transfer onto a baking sheet and roast for 15 minutes. Remove from oven, turn sweet potatoes over, and roast for another 10 minutes. Remove from oven again, reduce heat to 325°F (165°C), turn sweet potatoes over again, and roast for another 10–15 minutes.

Makes 4 servings.

Although these orange-fleshed sweet potatoes are often referred to as yams, "true" yams are actually unrelated to sweet potatoes, being a tropical tuber grown in Latin America and the Caribbean.

You may use any other root vegetable (e.g., yellow-fleshed sweet potatoes, acorn squash, celery root, beets) in this recipe, just ensure you adjust cooking according to the size and type of vegetable.

SEVEN-GRAIN RICE WITH CHICKPEAS & ROMANO BEANS

1 cup uncooked
seven-grain rice

3 cups chicken stock
(see note)

1 tsp paprika

1 tsp salt

1 can (18¼-oz/540-mL)
chickpeas (garbanzo
beans) (may use less if
desired)

1 can (18¼-oz/540-mL)
Romano beans (may use
less if desired) (see note)

½ medium onion, diced

1 clove garlic, minced

¼ cup fresh basil,
chopped

½ chives, chopped

½ cup fresh parsley,
chopped

½ cup olive oil

¼ cup red wine vinegar

At home, Alessandra often creates wonderful dishes using whatever ingredients are available in our refrigerator or pantry; this is one of them. Feel free to use any combination of beans you like. This can be served hot or cold. —JF.

In a large pot on high heat, combine rice and stock, and bring to a boil. Once boiling, reduce heat to low and stir in paprika and salt. Cover with a lid and simmer for 30–35 minutes, until rice is well-cooked and tender. In a large bowl, add remaining ingredients and mix until well combined. Add cooked rice to bean mixture, toss until well combined, and serve.

MAKES 6 SERVINGS.

FOR A VEGETARIAN VERSION, USE VEGETABLE STOCK OR WATER INSTEAD OF CHICKEN STOCK.

ROMANO BEANS, ALSO KNOWN AS BORLOTTI BEANS, ARE NOT TO BE CONFUSED WITH THE BROAD FLAT GREEN BEAN OF THE SAME NAME. THE ROMANOS USED IN THIS RECIPE ARE PULSES THAT ARE GENERALLY TAN OR A BROWN/PINKISH COLOUR WITH STREAKS, AND ARE OFTEN USED IN ITALIAN CUISINE.

Mushroom & Pearl Barley Risotto with Truffle Oil

....

Using pearl barley in risotto is a nice change from the traditional Arborio rice. It has a wonderful texture that is especially appealing to young, untrained palates! The mushrooms add an earthy, fragrant quality, but you could omit them if serving this with bold-tasting entrées.

In a medium-sized pot on medium, heat 2 tbsp olive oil. Add 1 tbsp garlic and sauté for 2 minutes, until softened. Add pearl barley and stir. Add 1 cup chicken stock and stir continually. As liquid reduces, add another cup of stock and continue to stir. Repeat with remaining 2 cups stock as liquid continues to reduce. In a separate pan on medium, heat remaining 2 tbsp olive oil. Add remaining 1 tbsp garlic and all mushrooms and sauté for 5–8 minutes, until softened. Season with salt and pepper. Transfer mushroom mixture to barley as it continues to cook, adding more stock if necessary. (Barley will take approximately 30-40 minutes total to cook.) When done, add butter and cheese and stir through; risotto should have a creamy consistency. Serve in a large bowl (or in individual portions), garnish with parsley, and drizzle a little truffle oil over top.

4 tbsp extra virgin olive oil

2 tbsp garlic, chopped

1 cup pearl barley

4 cups chicken stock (or more if needed)

2 cups mixed mushrooms (e.g., shiitake, oyster, button, chanterelles) (see note)

Salt to taste

Freshly ground black pepper to taste

½ small onion, chopped

¼ cup cold butter

¼ cup Romano or Parmesan cheese, grated

Fresh parsley, chopped (for garnish)

Truffle oil (for finishing) (see note)

Makes 4 servings.

You can include any of your favorite wild mushrooms in this recipe. Fresh ones are best, but some dried varieties are fine (e.g., shiitake, morel, and chanterelle). If using dried, reconstitute them in hot water.

Truffle oil is a traditional French and Italian delicacy created by soaking white or black truffles in olive oil. It has an earthy and robust aroma and flavor, and is even considered an aphrodisiac. Truffle oil is available at specialty and gourmet markets and some supermarkets.

New World Panisse

....

Panisse *is a baked or deep-fried chickpea-flour cake that is similar to polenta, but smoother in texture and with a nutty flavor. Serve warm on the side of a stew or as a side dish with any meat entrée.*

2 cups chickpea flour
(see note)

1½ qt (1½ L) whole milk

½ cup butter

1 tsp salt

1 tsp herbes de Provence
(see note on page 27)

2 cups canola oil
(for frying)

Lightly oil a 9-in (23-cm) square baking pan. In a large bowl, add flour and slowly whisk in milk and continue to whisk until flour is well incorporated. Strain mixture into a heavy-bottomed pot to remove unwanted lumps. Turn heat on medium and whisk in butter, salt, and herbes de Provence and continue to whisk until liquid comes to a boil and starts to thicken. Once boiling, continue to whisk for 3 minutes, then pour into baking pan, let cool, and refrigerate for 4 hours to set. Remove from refrigerator and slice panisse into 1-in (2½-cm) sticks then remove from pan with a spatula. In a large frying pan on medium-high, heat oil. Add panisse sticks and fry for about 4 minutes total, turning until all sides are browned.

Makes 4 servings.

Chickpea flour (also known as gram or channa flour) is available at most markets that sell bulk grains.

Soft Parmesan Polenta

....

1½ cups chicken stock

1½ cups whole milk

2 tsp salt

1 tsp black pepper

½ cup cornmeal

½ cup Parmesan cheese, grated (may use Romano)

Our sons Remi and Matisse absolutely love this recipe for soft polenta, the Italian staple made with cornmeal. Alessandra always makes extra because she knows they'll fight over it. Serve with the Braised Lamb Shanks with Tomato Sauce (page 156) or any roast or stew. —JF.

In a medium saucepan on medium-high heat, combine stock, milk, salt, and pepper and bring to a boil. Once boiling, reduce heat to medium-low and slowly stir in cornmeal with a whisk. Continue to whisk for 8–10 minutes, until mixture starts to bubble. Simmer for another 5 minutes, whisking continually, until polenta becomes smooth. If it gets too thick, add a little more water or milk. Remove from heat, stir in cheese, and serve.

MAKES 4 SERVINGS.

NONNA'S MANICOTTI

....

Manicotti was always a part of all-day Sunday dinners at my Nonna and Nonno's (Grandma and Grandpa's) house in Toronto when I grew up. Italians often enjoy pasta as an appetizer (prima platti) *rather than a main course. This is a nice, light recipe that my Nonna passed down to my father, which he then often prepared for me and my sisters. —A.*

Preheat oven to 350°F (180°C). In a large pot of boiling salted water, cook pasta noodles for 8–10 minutes. Strain and set noodles aside on an oiled platter. In a large bowl, combine ricotta cheese, ¼ cup Romano cheese, spinach, salt, and pepper and mix well. Gently whisk in egg and stir until well combined. On a flat surface, lay down cooked pasta noodles flat and spoon (or use piping bag) 3 tbsp of cheese mixture along one end of each pasta sheet, then roll up. Repeat until all cheese mixture is used. Place manicotti seam-side down into a casserole dish and cover with tomato sauce and cream. Bake for 25 minutes. Remove from oven, sprinkle remaining ½ cup Romano cheese over top, and serve.

MAKES 6 SERVINGS.

1 pkg fresh lasagna noodles, cut into 3×5-in (7½×13-cm) rectangles; or 20 fresh pasta squares

1½ lb (680 g) ricotta cheese

¾ cup Romano cheese

2 cups fresh spinach, chopped

1 tsp salt

1 tsp black pepper

1 large egg

3 cups Tomato Sauce (page 87)

¼ cup cream

Fresh parsley (for garnish)

Orecchiette Pasta with Rapini & Olives

....

I have fond memories of this pasta dish from Puglia, Italy, which my dad often cooks. Orecchiette means "little ears" (referring to the pasta's shape), which always makes our kids laugh! Rapini is a traditional Italian green leafy vegetable (also used in Chinese cuisine) that looks like a cross between kale and broccoli; their stalks have a bitter taste, so be sure to remove as much of them as possible, leaving mostly leaves. —A.

On high heat, bring a large pot of generously salted water to a rapid boil. Add pasta and cook according to package instructions until al dente. (Orecchiette pasta takes longer to cook than other pastas, so be sure to check the package.) Meanwhile, in a large frying pan on medium-high, heat oil. Add garlic, wine, and stock and cook for 3–4 minutes, stirring continually to allow liquid to reduce. Add rapini and anchovies to sauce, and cook for 3–4 minutes, until rapini is wilted. Add olives, salt, pepper, and butter and mix to incorporate. When done, strain, toss with sauce, and serve.

Makes 4 servings.

3 cups dry orecchiette pasta (if unavailable, use penne pasta)

2 tbsp olive oil

3 cloves garlic, chopped

¼ cup white wine (optional)

½ cup chicken stock

1 bunch fresh rapini, stalks removed and diced

6 filets anchovy (optional)

¼ cup green olives or sun-dried black olives, pitted, halved or leave whole

Salt to taste

Freshly ground black pepper to taste

1 tbsp butter

Warm Potato Salad with L'Ancienne Mustard Vinaigrette

VINAIGRETTE:

1 tbsp L'Ancienne (whole-grain) mustard

1 tsp Dijon mustard

1 clove garlic, chopped

¼ cup red or white wine vinegar

½ cup extra virgin olive oil

½ tsp salt

½ tsp black pepper

2 tbsp extra virgin olive oil

2 stalks green onions, chopped

½ medium onion, sliced

2 lbs baby new potatoes, cooked then quartered

This is a great light alternative to regular potato salad. L'Ancienne mustard is the traditional whole-grain mustard. Serving this salad warm enhances its flavor and texture. It is wonderful accompanying a fish entrée, or as part of brunch.

TO PREPARE VINAIGRETTE: In a bowl, combine mustards, garlic, and vinegar. Slowly whisk in oil and continue to whisk until emulsified. Season with salt and pepper and taste test, adding more vinegar or oil if desired.

In a frying pan on medium heat, heat oil. Add green onions and onions and sauté for 1 minute, then add potatoes and sauté for 3–4 minutes, until cooked through. Transfer to a bowl and let cool slightly. Drizzle vinaigrette over top, mix to incorporate, and serve.

MAKES 4 SERVINGS.

Fish & Seafood Mains

Bouillabaisse

Lingcod aux Epices

Tapenade-Crusted Lingcod

Fennel Pollen-Dusted Wild Salmon
with Lemon Aïoli

Seared Rockfish with Artichoke
& Roasted Red Pepper

Grilled Halibut with Cherry
Tomato-Coriander Vinaigrette

Seared Yellowfin Tuna à la Provence

Roasted Dungeness Crab
with Virgin Sauce

Seared Scallops with Snow Pea
Sprouts & Mediterranean Vinaigrette

Scallop Brochettes aux Epices

Prawns Provençal

Prawn & Scallop Brochettes
with L'Ancienne Mustard
& Lemon Vinaigrette

Sautéed Tiger Prawns
with Socca Galettes

Seafood Linguini

BOUILLABAISSE

....

Most restaurants in the South of France require 48-hour notice to order a traditional bouillabaisse. The soup is a beautiful presentation of fresh Mediterranean fish traditionally accompanied by croutons and rouille *(garlic saffron mayo). In this recipe, we shorten the cooking process and serve everything in one bowl. Prepare the Fish Soup (page 67) a few days early to save time; once potatoes are cooked and fish is cubed, the actual cooking is quick and easy. Serve with Rouille (page 82), grated Gruyère cheese, and Crostini (page 69) on the side (see note).*

In a large pot on high heat, bring fish soup to a boil. Add fish, mussels, and clams and let soup return to a boil, then add potatoes, prawns, and scallops. After 2 minutes, once prawns have turned pink, turn off heat. Discard any mussels or clams that have not opened. Drizzle oil over top, and sprinkle with fresh herbs. Serve in individual bowls.

MAKES 4 SERVINGS.

JUST BEFORE SAVORING THIS BOUILLABAISSE, YOU CAN ADD ROUILLE, CHEESE, AND CROSTINI DIRECTLY INTO SOUP INSTEAD OF SERVING THEM ON THE SIDE, LETTING THE CHEESE MELT INTO THE BROTH.

PURCHASE THE FRESHEST MUSSELS AND CLAMS POSSIBLE FROM YOUR LOCAL SEAFOOD MARKET, CHOOSING ONES THAT ARE CLOSED TIGHTLY AND DISCARDING ANY THAT ARE OPEN OR BROKEN. FRESH MUSSELS AND CLAMS MUST BE STORED IN THE REFRIGERATOR AND COOKED THE SAME DAY OF PURCHASE.

5 cups Fish Soup
(page 67)

8 pieces (2½-oz/70-g each) fresh seasonal fish (e.g., halibut, salmon, ling cod, sablefish, or a combination)

½ lb (225 g) mussels, cleaned and de-bearded (see note)

½ lb (225 g) clams, cleaned (see note)

1 cup potatoes, boiled and sliced

8 fresh large prawns, peeled (tails left on) and deveined

8 fresh large bay scallops

⅛ cup extra virgin olive oil

¼ cup fresh herbs (e.g., chives, parsley, and basil), chopped

LINGCOD AUX EPICES

1 tsp ground star anise

1 tsp cinnamon

1 tsp ground fennel seeds

2 tsp celery salt

1 tsp ground coriander seeds

¼ cup olive oil

4 filets (6-oz/170-g each) lingcod

1 tsp salt

The mixture of these spices inspired by Middle Eastern cuisine adds unique flavor to this somewhat underrated Pacific coast fish. Lingcod is perfect for people new at cooking fish because it has a richer texture and doesn't overcook as easily as other fish do. Serve with a fresh salad or boiled potatoes on the side.

In a small bowl, combine star anise, cinnamon, fennel seeds, celery salt, and coriander seeds. In a frying pan on medium-high, heat oil. Coat each piece of fish in spice mixture, sprinkle with salt, then place flesh-side down in pan. Sear each fish for 6–8 minutes on each side, then remove and blot any excess oil with a paper towel. Place on a platter and serve.

MAKES 4 SERVINGS.

TAPENADE-CRUSTED LINGCOD

·····················

Here's another wonderful recipe for lingcod; they're not the prettiest-looking fish but they are unique to the Pacific West Coast. Lingcod's mild flavor and dense white flesh lends itself very well to the saltiness of the tapenade.

Preheat oven to 450°F (230°C). Place peppers on baking sheet and roast for about 25 minutes until blackened, turning occasionally to roast evenly. Remove from oven and place in a plastic bag to cool completely. Remove skins (they should come off easily), discard seeds, and slice lengthwise into strips. This can be done a day in advance and stored in the refrigerator.

Preheat oven to 425°F (220°C). In a frying pan on high, heat ¼ cup oil. Season lingcod filets with ½ tsp salt and sear skin-side only, for about 3 minutes, until skin is crispy and brown (this may need to be done in batches). Remove and place on a baking sheet. Spread 1 tbsp tapenade on each filet and bake for 6–8 minutes, until flesh separates from bones easily. In a separate frying pan on medium-high, heat remaining ¼ cup oil. Add fennel and sauté for about 5 minutes, until soft (reduce heat if necessary). Add roasted peppers and remaining ½ tsp salt and sauté for 1–2 minutes, until peppers are heated through. For each serving, place 3 potato halves on each plate and beside them spoon 2 tbsp fennel-pepper mixture; place a tapenade-crusted lingcod filet on top.

MAKES 4 SERVINGS.

3 whole red bell peppers

½ cup olive oil

4 filets (6-oz/170-g each) lingcod

1 tsp salt

4 tbsp Tapenade (page 64)

2 fennel bulbs, thinly sliced

6 baby new potatoes, boiled and halved

½ cup fresh herbs (e.g., chive, basil, parsley), chopped

Fennel Pollen-Dusted Wild Salmon with Lemon Aïoli

We were inspired to create this dish when our specialty mushroom supplier Tyler Gray of Mikuni Wild Harvest showed up at the restaurant one day with a new product, fennel pollen. It's incredible—like taking fennel seeds and intensifying them a hundred times over. It adds bright bursts of flavor to anything, from vegetables to roast chicken, and is great when sprinkled on salads or mixed with a little extra virgin olive oil for dipping bread. We've used it here with salmon to create a very romantic partnership! This recipe includes directions to make roasted potatoes and sautéed snap peas, for the perfect meal.

TO PREPARE LEMON AÏOLI: In a food processor, combine egg yolk, mustard, and garlic, and purée until egg and mustard are blended together. Add salt and pepper. Purée again while slowly adding oil, and continue to purée until ingredients are emulsified. Add lemon zest and juice and pulse until incorporated. Cover and refrigerate until needed; may be stored in refrigerator for up to 3 days.

Preheat oven to 375°F (190°C). In a large bowl, toss potatoes with ⅛ cup oil, butter, garlic, and half the salt and pepper. Place in a roasting pan and roast for 30–40 minutes, until golden brown. Remove and set aside. Increase oven temperature to 400°F (205°C). On a clean work surface, season fish with remaining salt and pepper. Evenly distribute fennel pollen on one side of salmon (if using filets with skin, distribute pollen over flesh side). In a sauté pan on

(continued)

LEMON AÏOLI:

1 egg yolk

2 tsp Dijon mustard

1 tsp garlic, chopped

¼ tsp salt

¼ tsp black pepper

1 cup olive oil

Zest of ½ lemon (zest lemon before juicing, see below)

2 tbsp lemon juice

4 medium Yukon Gold potatoes, quartered lengthwise

¼ cup + 2 tbsp olive oil

1 tsp garlic, chopped

1 tsp butter

1 tsp salt

½ tsp black pepper

4 filets (6-oz/170-g each) wild salmon

3 tsp fennel pollen (see notes)

40 whole snap peas, strings removed

medium to high heat, add another ⅛ cup oil and allow to heat for about 30 seconds until hot, then sear salmon, pollen-side down, for 2–3 minutes. Immediately place in a baking pan, pollen-side up, and bake for 5–8 minutes. Remove from oven and set aside. Meanwhile, in another sauté pan on medium to high, heat remaining 2 tbsp oil. Add snap peas, season with salt and pepper as desired, and sauté for 1 minute. Add potatoes and toss quickly until reheated and combined with snap peas. Serve immediately alongside salmon, with lemon aïoli on the side.

MAKES 4 SERVINGS.

NO MATTER WHERE YOU LIVE, MANY MARKETS AND FISHMONGERS SELL FRESH WILD SALMON, SO YOU DON'T HAVE TO LIVE ON THE WEST COAST IN ORDER TO ENJOY IT.

FENNEL POLLEN IS A SPICE THAT IS CONSIDERED A DELICACY, SIMILAR TO SAFFRON——A LITTLE GOES A LONG WAY. IT IS AVAILABLE AT MOST GOURMET MARKETS OR SPECIALTY FOOD DISTRIBUTORS. ALTHOUGH FENNEL POLLEN'S TASTE IS DISTINCT FROM FENNEL SEEDS, YOU MAY SUBSTITUTE IT WITH GROUND FENNEL SEEDS IF NEEDED.

SEARED ROCKFISH WITH ARTICHOKE & ROASTED RED PEPPER

....

Rockfish, or rascasse *as it's known in the Mediterranean, is similar to red snapper. Its flaky, medium-firm texture makes it an easy fish to prepare. Generally, rockfish has a sweet, mild flavor, and is best baked, sautéed, broiled or poached, but is not ideal for grilling.*

Set oven to broil. Place pepper under broiler to roast until black, turning occasionally so all sides roast evenly. Remove from oven and place in a plastic bag to let cool completely. Remove skin from pepper (it should come off easily), discard seeds, and slice lengthwise into strips. Cut artichokes in half and season with ¼ tsp salt and ¼ tsp black pepper. In a barbecue or under an oven broiler, grill or broil artichokes until golden brown, and set aside. Set oven temperature to 400°F (205°C). Lightly oil a baking sheet with ⅛ cup oil. In a large bowl, combine bell peppers, artichokes, olives, garlic, and another ¼ cup oil, ½ tsp salt, and ½ tsp black pepper and mix well. In a frying pan on high heat, melt butter. Place fish skin-side down in pan and sear skin-side only for about 2 minutes, until skin is slightly crispy. Transfer fish skin-side down on baking sheet and bake for 5–7 minutes. To serve, evenly portion artichoke mixture in center of plates. Gently place 2 filets on each plate, drizzle with remaining ⅛ cup oil, and sprinkle with fresh herbs.

MAKES 4 SERVINGS.

1 large red bell pepper

1 can (13½-oz/400-mL) artichokes packed in water

¾ tsp salt

¾ tsp black pepper

⅓ cup black olives (Kalamatas are good), pitted and chopped

1 tsp garlic, chopped

½ cup extra virgin olive oil

1 tbsp butter

4 filets (6-oz/170-g each) rockfish, cleaned

¼ cup extra virgin olive oil (for finishing)

¼ cup fresh herbs (e.g., basil, chives, parsley), chopped

GRILLED HALIBUT WITH CHERRY TOMATO-CORIANDER VINAIGRETTE

....

This recipe is best served from March to November, when halibut is in season. See below for a variation of this recipe that substitutes a tapenade for the vinaigrette (the halibut and tapenade version of this recipe is featured on the photo on the oppoiste page).

TO PREPARE VINAIGRETTE: In a pot of boiling water, blanch tomatoes for 5–10 seconds, then immediately place in a bowl of ice water to halt cooking process. Remove skins and place in a bowl with basil, garlic, salt, pepper, and coriander, and mix well. Cover and let marinate at room temperature for 1 hour.

TO PREPARE POTATOES: In a large pot, combine water and saffron and let sit to infuse for 30 minutes, then place on medium-high heat. When saffron water is simmering, add potatoes and cook for 5–8 minutes, until just tender. Drain and place potatoes in a metal bowl to keep warm. (This can be done in advance; reheat potatoes in microwave or oven just before serving.)

TO PREPARE ASPARAGUS: Set barbecue or stovetop grill to a medium-high heat (see note). In a baking dish, add asparagus and drizzle with oil, then season with salt and pepper. Grill for 4 minutes, turning to ensure it cooks evenly, until tender. Set aside and keep warm.

(continued)

VINAIGRETTE (see note):

2 cups cherry tomatoes

Ice water

2 cups fresh basil, chopped

1 tbsp garlic, chopped

1 tsp salt

1 tsp black pepper

1 tsp coriander seeds, crushed

POTATOES:

4 cups water

2 pinches saffron threads

8 new potatoes, sliced ½-in (1-cm) thick

ASPARAGUS:

20 large asparagus (see note)

2 tbsp olive oil

Salt to taste

Freshly ground black pepper to taste

Canola oil (for coating grill)

FISH (see note):

4 filets (6-oz/170-g each) fresh halibut

¼ cup olive oil

1 tsp salt

1 tsp freshly ground black pepper

TO PREPARE FISH: Preheat oven to 425°F (220°C). Place frying pan on high heat. Coat fish in oil and place fish skin-side down, season with salt and pepper, and cook for 3 minutes, then turn over, season with salt and pepper, and place flesh-side down in a baking dish. Bake for 5 minutes. To serve: on each plate, place 5 asparagus, arrange potatoes across bottom half of asparagus, top with a piece of fish, and drizzle vinaigrette evenly around and over all.

MAKES 4 SERVINGS.

INSTEAD OF THE VINAIGRETTE, YOU CAN MIX ½ CUP TAPENADE (PAGE 73) AND ¼ CUP EXTRA VIRGIN OLIVE OIL IN A BOWL UNTIL WELL COMBINED.

SELECT ASPARAGUS THAT HAVE FIRM, CRISP STALKS OF EVEN THICKNESS, WITH TIGHTLY CLOSED TIPS. YOUNG ASPARAGUS NEEDS ONLY THE WOODY STEM SNAPPED OFF; HOWEVER, OLDER ASPARAGUS MAY NEED PEELING.

YOU MAY BLANCH ASPARAGUS INSTEAD OF GRILLING THEM: PLACE IN BOILING SALTED WATER FOR ABOUT 1 MINUTE (NO LONGER) TO MAINTAIN THEIR CRISPNESS AND BRIGHT GREEN COLOR. SUBMERGE IN ICE-COLD WATER TO HALT THE COOKING PROCESS.

INSTEAD OF HALIBUT, YOU CAN SUBSTITUTE SABLEFISH (ALSO KNOWN AS ALASKAN BLACK COD).

Seared Yellowfin Tuna à la Provence

....

This recipe is similar to the Seared Scallops with Snow Pea Sprouts (page 128), but with the addition of fresh tomatoes and herbs for that Provençal touch. We use yellowfin tuna here, but any type of fresh tuna will work (but try to choose sustainable varieties). This dish should be served immediately, and be sure that it is not overcooked. Serve alongside basmati rice.

TO PREPARE SAUCE: In a bowl, combine sun-dried tomatoes, olives, fennel, capers, basil, and ¼ cup + 2 tbsp oil. Mix until well combined, then set aside. In a medium pan on medium-high, heat remaining 2 tbsp oil. Add tomatoes, garlic, salt, and pepper and sauté for 2–3 minutes. Add sun-dried tomato mixture, mix until heated through, then remove from heat.

Season tuna with salt and pepper. In a large pan on high, heat oil. Sear tuna for 1 minute on each side (no longer), then immediately remove fish from pan (it will continue to cook once removed). Place fish on a platter and pour sauce on top, or arrange each piece on individual plates and distribute sauce evenly.

MAKES 4 SERVINGS.

SAUCE:

¼ cup oil-packed sun-dried tomatoes (if using dried form, reconstitute in hot water), minced

¼ cup Kalamata olives, pitted and minced

¼ cup fennel bulb, minced

¼ cup capers, minced

¼ cup fresh basil, sliced

½ cup extra virgin olive oil

1 cup tomatoes, chopped

3 cloves garlic, chopped

Salt to taste

Freshly ground black pepper to taste

1 tbsp extra virgin olive oil

4 filets (6-oz/170-g each) fresh yellowfin tuna

1 tsp salt

½ tsp black pepper

Roasted Dungeness Crab with Virgin Sauce

....

I will never forget the first time Jean-Francis took me on a date to a restaurant, a small bistro in Vieux (Old) Nice. On display in front of the restaurant was a large, enticing array of fresh seafood, inspiring Jean-Francis to order two crabs that were simply boiled and served with mayonnaise. We devoured both of them, savoring every last scrumptious morsel; no forks were needed. I'm sure that we were a real sight to be seen with our messy hands and faces! To this day, we still enjoy crab, which we roast for intimate dinner parties at home. It takes time and patience to eat crab, which gives you time to socialize with your guests. —A.

Preheat oven to 375°F (190°C). In a large roasting pan, place crab pieces, then distribute remaining ingredients evenly over them. Roast for 30–40 minutes, until crab is slightly brown around edges and the ingredients around the crab are golden and caramelized.

Makes 4 servings.

When using live crab, you may find it easier to have it cleaned and cut up for you at the market; be sure to cook it on the same day that you purchase it.

4 (2-lb/900-g each) whole Dungeness crabs, cleaned, heads removed, and cut into 8 pieces (see note)

2 cups Virgin Sauce (page 86)

¼ cup butter, chopped

½ cup white wine

1 tsp salt

1 tsp black pepper

2 tbsp fresh ginger, chopped

¼ cup extra virgin olive oil

Seared Scallops with Snow Pea Sprouts & Mediterranean Vinaigrette

....

VINAIGRETTE:

¼ cup sun-dried tomatoes, minced

¼ cup black olives, minced

¼ fennel bulb, minced

2 tbsp capers, minced

½ cup extra virgin olive oil

¼ cup + 2 tbsp olive oil

20 fresh bay scallops, muscles removed and patted dry

4 cups snow pea sprouts

2 tsp garlic, chopped

1 tsp salt

1 tsp black pepper

4 tsp crema di balsamico (see note)

You cannot afford to make mistakes with these pricey delicacies. Chewing on an overcooked scallop is worse than chewing on a piece of my sons' ABC (already been chewed) gum! For this recipe, look for the large, plump bay scallops that are slightly sweeter than smaller varieties (which you can use if bay scallops are not available); they should weigh approximately 2 oz (60 g) each. Remember to always remove the tough muscle attached to each scallop before using (they may already have been removed at the fish market). This dish can also be served in smaller portions as an appetizer. —A.

In a bowl, combine all vinaigrette ingredients and mix until well combined, then set aside. In a frying pan on high, heat ¼ cup oil. Add scallops and sear for 2 minutes on each side, then immediately remove from pan and set aside. In the same pan on medium, heat another 2 tbsp oil. Add snow pea sprouts, garlic, salt, and pepper and sauté for 3 minutes. To serve, place sprouts in center of a large serving platter and surround with scallops. Drizzle vinaigrette over scallops, and creatively drizzle crema di balsamico on sides of platter.

MAKES 4 SERVINGS.

YOU CAN PURCHASE A BALSAMIC REDUCTION ALSO KNOWN AS *CREMA DI BALSAMICO* AT SPECIALTY FOOD SHOPS. OR, TO MAKE YOUR OWN: IN A SAUCEPAN ON HIGH HEAT, BRING 1 CUP INEXPENSIVE BALSAMIC VINEGAR TO A BOIL, THEN REDUCE HEAT TO MEDIUM FOR ABOUT 10 MINUTES OR UNTIL IT REDUCES TO ¼ CUP. LET COOL BEFORE USING, AND REFRIGERATE LEFTOVERS.

Scallop Brochettes aux Epices

....

This spice mix is delicious with scallops. We taught this recipe to over 150 people on an Alaskan cruise one year and it was served as part of the ship's dinner menu one night. It was a huge success and the passengers gave it rave reviews. This recipe requires 8 bamboo skewers, pre-soaked; if you don't have any, you can gently sauté the scallops instead.

Preheat oven to 400°F (205°C). In a small bowl, combine celery salt, star anise, coriander seeds, cinnamon, and fennel seeds. In a large frying pan on medium-high, heat ¼ cup oil. Sear scallops for about 1 minute on each side—do not cook all the way through. Remove from pan, let cool slightly, then place 4 scallops on each skewer. Dust with spice mixture and place on a baking sheet. Bake scallops for 2–3 minutes maximum. In a separate frying pan on medium-high, heat remaining ¼ cup oil. Add zucchini, salt, pepper, and garlic, and sauté, stirring continually, until zucchini is softened. Add basil and stir to mix. To serve, distribute zucchini evenly in center of each plate. Place skewers on top (2 per serving) and drizzle with extra virgin olive oil.

MAKES 4 SERVINGS.

TO PREPARE THE ZUCCHINI, SLICE OPEN LENGTHWISE AND THEN SCOOP OUT THE INNER WHITE PART WITH SEEDS WITH A SPOON (YOU CAN SAVE THIS FOR SOUPS). WITH A MANDOLIN SLICER OR KNIFE, JULIENNE THE REMAINING OUTER FLESH AND SKIN OF THE ZUCCHINI.

2 tsp celery salt

1 tsp ground star anise

1 tsp ground coriander seeds

1 tsp cinnamon

1 tsp ground fennel seeds

½ cup olive oil

20 fresh large bay scallops, muscle removed and patted dry

4 small–medium zucchini, de-seeded and julienned (see note)

1 tsp salt

1 tsp black pepper

1 tbsp garlic, chopped

¼ cup fresh basil leaves, chopped

¼ cup extra virgin olive oil (for finishing)

PRAWNS PROVENÇAL

....

The French typically eat these prawns with the heads and tails, where all the flavor resides (our kids love them). Try it if you and your guests are feeling a little French! This recipe requires a gas stove to flambé the prawns; if you have an electric stove, you will need matches. (Don't worry, the alcohol burns off quickly.) Serve with green vegetables and Seven-Grain Rice with Chickpeas & Romano Beans (page 104).

2 tbsp olive oil

2 tbsp butter

2 tbsp garlic, chopped

32 fresh medium–large prawns, peeled and deveined (unpeeled, if you prefer)

Salt to taste

Freshly ground black pepper to taste

¼ cup brandy

¼ cup fresh parsley, chopped

2 tsp freshly squeezed lemon juice

PREPARE PRAWNS IN 2 BATCHES: In a large sauté pan on medium-high, heat 1 tbsp oil and 1 tbsp butter. Add 1 tbsp garlic and sauté for 1 minute. Increase heat to high, add half the prawns, season with salt and pepper, and sauté for 2 minutes on each side until they turn just pink—do not overcook. Then, to flambé with brandy: with one hand, remove pan from heat and with the other hand, pour in ⅛ cup brandy. Quickly bring pan back to the heat (see note). If you have a gas stove, carefully tilt pan toward flame and it will flambé automatically; if you have an electric stove, light a match and carefully put the flame close to the pan to allow it to catch fire. Let flames dissipate on their own. Sprinkle with ⅛ cup parsley over prawns, drizzle with lemon juice, and stir to combine, then transfer to a serving platter. Repeat process with remaining ingredients.

MAKES 4 SERVINGS.

IF PAN IS NOT HOT ENOUGH, THE BRANDY WILL NOT IGNITE, SO MAKE SURE THE PAN GETS NICE AND HOT.

THIS DISH CAN ALSO BE SERVED AS AN APPETIZER; GUESTS WILL LOVE TO WATCH THEM BEING PREPARED, THEN LOVE TO NIBBLE ON THEM!

PRAWN & SCALLOP BROCHETTES WITH L'ANCIENNE MUSTARD & LEMON VINAIGRETTE

....

VINAIGRETTE:

3 tbsp L'Ancienne mustard (see note)

Juice of 1 lemon

1 dash Tabasco

1 dash Worcestershire sauce

2 tsp honey

⅔ cup extra virgin olive oil

Salt to taste

Freshly ground black pepper to taste

16 medium tiger prawns, skins removed (keep tails on) and deveined

16 medium scallops, muscles removed and patted dry

1 tbsp olive oil (for prawns and scallops)

1¼ tsp salt

1¼ tsp black pepper

6 new potatoes, cooked and halved

2 tbsp + ¼ cup extra virgin olive oil

1 tbsp garlic, chopped

24 cherry tomatoes

1 lb (450 g) spinach leaves, washed and dried

¼ cup fresh herbs of your choice, chopped

Here is another way to prepare scallops, with prawns. It is better to skewer scallops lengthwise so that they lay flat while on the grill. The mustard and lemon vinaigrette is a nice, light sauce ideal for summer barbecues. This recipe requires 8 bamboo skewers, pre-soaked.

TO PREPARE VINAIGRETTE: In a bowl, combine mustard, lemon juice, Tabasco, and Worcestershire sauce and mix well. Stir in honey and oil, mixing until emulsified. Season with salt and pepper and set aside.

TO PREPARE BROCHETTES: Preheat oven to 375° F (190°C). Prepare 4 skewers with only prawns (4 prawns each) and 4 skewers with only scallops (4 scallops each). Rub with 1 tbsp olive oil and season with ½ tsp salt and ½ tsp pepper. In a barbecue on high heat or in a very hot frying pan, sear prawn and scallop brochettes (in batches if necessary) for 1 minute each side—do not cook through. Set aside on a baking sheet. Place potatoes in bowl, season with another ½ tsp salt and ½ tsp pepper, and drizzle with 2 tbsp extra virgin olive oil. On a barbecue, grill potatoes for about 2 minutes to give them grill marks (or fry in a frying pan on stovetop). Set on baking sheet alongside brochettes. In a large frying pan on medium-high, heat remaining

¼ cup extra virgin olive oil. Add garlic, tomatoes, and remaining ¼ tsp salt and ¼ tsp pepper, and sauté for 2–3 minutes. Meanwhile, bake brochettes and potatoes in oven for 3–5 minutes. Add spinach to tomato mixture and toss for 1 minute, until spinach is just wilted. To serve, place spinach-tomato mixture in center of a platter and surround with potatoes and brochettes. Drizzle with vinaigrette and sprinkle brochettes with herbs.

MAKES 4 SERVINGS.

MUSTARDS THAT ARE *L'ANCIENNE*, MEANING "OLD-FASHIONED," ARE GRAINY MUSTARDS BECAUSE TRADITIONALLY, MUSTARDS ARE WHOLE GRAIN, NOT SMOOTH LIKE TODAY.

SAUTÉED TIGER PRAWNS WITH SOCCA GALETTES

This recipe combines the bounty of the ocean with traditional socca galettes. *Its starchy versatility is a welcome change from rice or potatoes. If you want to try something a little different, this is sure to please. It is best to prepare the tomato and onion mélange first, and while it is cooking, prepare the galettes and then the prawns just before the mélange is ready.*

TO PREPARE MÉLANGE: In a frying pan on medium, heat oil. Add onions, salt, pepper, and herbes de Provence and allow onions to sweat for about 3 minutes, until onions are almost translucent. Add tomatoes and garlic, stir to combine, reduce heat to low and simmer for 25–30 minutes, stirring occasionally.

TO PREPARE GALETTES: In a bowl, combine flour, salt, and sugar. Whisk in eggs, then slowly pour in milk while continuing to whisk. Strain if there are too many lumps. In a frying pan on medium heat, add 1 tsp melted butter. Spoon a 2-tbsp dollop of batter into pan and cook for 2 minutes on each side. Transfer to a plate and cover with a tea towel to keep warm. Repeat process until all batter is used.

(continued)

TOMATO & ONION MÉLANGE:

½ cup olive oil

1 medium onion, sliced

1 tsp salt

½ tsp black pepper

1 tsp herbes de Provence (see note on page 27)

4 Roma tomatoes, peeled, seeded, and cut in ⅛ths

2 cloves garlic, chopped

GALETTES:

⅔ cup chickpea flour (see note)

1 dash salt

1 dash sugar

2 eggs

½ cup milk

¼ cup butter, melted

PRAWNS:

¼ cup olive oil

20 large tiger prawns, skins removed (keep tails on) and deveined

1 tsp salt

½ tsp black pepper

2 tbsp fresh basil, julienned

TO PREPARE PRAWNS: In a frying pan on high, heat ¼ cup olive oil. Season prawns with salt and pepper and sauté for about 3 minutes, until they just turn pink—do not overcook. Remove from heat.

TO SERVE: Arrange galettes on a large serving platter, place prawns on top, pour tomato and onion confit over top and around platter, and sprinkle with basil.

MAKES 4 SERVINGS.

CHICKPEA FLOUR (ALSO KNOWN AS GRAM OR CHANNA FLOUR) IS AVAILABLE AT MOST MARKETS THAT SELL BULK GRAINS.

Seafood Linguini

....

If you like pasta with fresh seafood, you'll love this simple recipe. The linguini absorbs the flavors of the mussels and clams, and, when combined with the rich tomato sauce, is a tasty treat for all seafood lovers.

Preheat oven to 350°F (180°C). In a large bowl, combine fish and prawns, coat with ¼ cup olive oil, and season with salt. In a grill pan on high heat, grill fish (in batches if necessary) about 1 minute on each side, then set aside. Grill prawns for 2 minutes on each side until they just turn pink—do not overcook—then set aside. In a large pot on medium, heat ⅛ cup extra virgin olive oil. Add mussels, clams, and garlic and sauté for 5 minutes, until garlic starts to brown. Add butter, wine, and tomato sauce, and stir continually, letting wine and tomato sauce reduce until mussels and clams start to open (discard any that do not open). Meanwhile, place fish and prawns in a baking dish and finishing cooking them in oven for 2 minutes.

(continued)

8 pieces fresh seasonal fish (e.g., halibut, salmon, tuna, or a combination), cut into 2-in (5-cm) cubes

8 fresh large prawns (e.g., spot or tiger prawns), peeled and deveined

¼ cup olive oil (to coat seafood)

1 tsp salt

⅛ cup extra virgin olive oil (for sautéing)

1 lb (455 g) mussels, bearded and cleaned (see note)

1 lb (455 g) clams, cleaned (see note)

2 tbsp garlic, minced

¼ butter

½ cup white wine

4 cups Tomato Sauce (page 87)

⅛ cup extra virgin olive oil (for finishing)

16 oz (450 g) linguini noodles, cooked (see note)

½ cup fresh mixed herbs (e.g., chives, parsley, and basil), chopped

Add freshly cooked noodles to sauce. Toss, coating pasta in sauce and immediately remove from heat. To serve, distribute pasta evenly into 4 pasta bowls, top with cooked fish and prawns, drizzle with oil, and sprinkle with herbs.

MAKES 4 SERVINGS.

PURCHASE THE FRESHEST MUSSELS AND CLAMS POSSIBLE FROM YOUR LOCAL SEAFOOD MARKET, CHOOSING ONES THAT ARE CLOSED TIGHTLY AND DISCARDING ANY THAT ARE OPEN OR BROKEN. FRESH MUSSELS AND CLAMS MUST BE STORED IN THE REFRIGERATOR AND COOKED THE SAME DAY OF PURCHASE.

THIS RECIPE CALLS FOR ABOUT 4-OZ (110-G) PASTA PER SERVING. COOK LINGUINE ACCORDING TO PACKAGE DIRECTIONS. FOR THIS RECIPE, COORDINATE THE COOKING TIME SO THAT THE PASTA IS READY JUST BEFORE IT'S SUPPOSED TO BE ADDED TO THE MUSSELS, CLAMS, AND SAUCE.

Meat Mains

Daube de Boeuf

Slow-Roasted Duck with
Fig Demi-Glace

Seared Beef Tenderloin with Red
Wine & Peppercorn Jus

Dijon-Roasted Chicken

Roast Chicken with Herbes de
Provence

Grilled Quail with Juniper Berry Jus

Whole Barbecued Rabbit

Matisse's Favorite Rabbit Stew with
Baby Carrots & Bacon

Mamie Suzanne's Pork Pot Roast

Fragrant Curried Pork

Involtini di Vitello (Italian Veal
Stuffed with Spinach & Mozzarella)

Braised Lamb Shanks
with Tomato Sauce

Rack of Lamb with Dijon-Herb Crust

Leg of Lamb Stuffed
with Olive Tapenade

Ragoût d'Agneau

Lamb Sirloin with Curried Israeli
Couscous

Daube de Boeuf

This is a French beef stew that is braised in a wine broth which is later reduced and served alongside the meat and vegetables. It's a classic Provençal recipe that has been passed down from generation to generation in our family. Here, we give you Mamie Suzanne's version that in 1987 won first prize from the Comité National de la Gastronomie in France, an association dedicated to promoting French gastronomy and its traditions through local and international demonstrations and competitions. This recipe requires fine string for tying the bouquet garni. Serve alongside steamed baby carrots and fresh fettuccini.

TO PREPARE BOUQUET GARNI: On 1 piece of leek, place bay leaf, thyme, parsley, and celery. Cover with other piece of leek and tie securely with fine string, leaving a length of string attached so that it can be easily retrieved.

In a large bowl, combine remaining ingredients except oil and stir until well combined, using enough wine to completely cover meat. Cover and refrigerate overnight to marinate. The next day, strain marinade into a bowl through a sieve and set liquid aside. Separate meat from remaining vegetable mixture. In a frying pan on high,

(continued)

BOUQUET GARNI:

2 (4-in/10-cm) pieces leek, green part only

1 bay leaf

3 sprigs fresh thyme

4 large sprigs fresh parsley

1 stalk (4-in/10-cm) celery

3 lb (1½ kg) boneless beef shank, cut into large cubes

3 medium onions, diced

3 carrots, diced

5 cloves garlic

4 whole cloves

3 cups + 1 tbsp (750 mL) red wine (more or less as needed) (see note)

1 piece dried orange peel (see note)

½ cup olive oil

3 cups demi-glace (see note)

heat oil. Add meat, in batches if necessary, and sear for about 1 minute on each side, until all sides are browned. Transfer seared meat to a large pot on medium heat and add reserved liquid, demiglace, and vegetable mixture. Cover with lid and bring to a simmer for 2½–3 hours, making sure it does not boil.

MAKES 6 SERVINGS.

TO DRY ORANGE PEEL: USING A KNIFE, CAREFULLY REMOVE A ½-IN (1-CM) THICK STRIP OF RIND FROM THE CIRCUMFERENCE OF AN ORANGE; AVOID THE BITTER WHITE PITH. PLACE RIND ON A PLATE NEAR A WINDOW TO DRY FOR 1–2 DAYS. LET YOUR FAMILY KNOW NOT TO THROW IT OUT!

DEMI-GLACE IS A TRADITIONAL FRENCH BROWN SAUCE MADE WITH BEEF OR VEAL STOCK, SHERRY, AND ESPAGNOLE SAUCE. FOR HOME COOKS, IT'S EASIER TO PURCHASE IT; IT CAN BE FOUND AT ANY SPECIALTY MARKET. IT MAY BE SUBSTITUTED WITH ORGANIC BEEF STOCK.

MAMIE SUZANNE BELIEVES THAT BECAUSE THIS RECIPE IS VERY RUSTIC, YOU NEED A RUSTIC CÔTE DU RHÔNE WINE FOR THE MARINADE. ALSO SERVE THIS DISH WITH A RED WINE THAT IS WELL-ROUNDED AND AT LEAST 5–8 YEARS OLD.

Slow-Roasted Duck with Fig Demi-Glace

....

Duck is perhaps not something you'd make at home, preferring instead to order it at your favorite Chinese restaurant. But the French love fowl in their cuisine, and duck is no exception. The fresh figs add sweetness to the demi-glace. So don't be shy; try something new!

Preheat oven to 320°F (160°C). On a rack in a large roasting pan, place ducks bone-side down, ensuring they do not touch bottom of pan. Sprinkle with salt and pepper. Roast uncovered for 2½–3 hours, until skin is golden brown and meat is falling off bones (if meat is getting too dark, cover ducks with lid or aluminium foil to roast for remaining 30 minutes if needed). Remove from oven and place on a serving platter. In a saucepan on medium heat, melt butter. Add figs and sauté for 2 minutes. Add demi-glace and cook for 2 minutes, stirring continually, then serve alongside duck.

Makes 4 servings.

You may substitute dried figs for fresh figs, but if you do, place them in roasting pan alongside duck to absorb juices while duck roasts, and omit the sautéing step.

Demi-glace is a traditional French brown sauce made with beef or veal stock, sherry, and espagnole sauce. For home cooks, it's easier to purchase it; it can be found at any specialty market. It may be substituted with organic beef stock.

2 whole ducks (about 5 lb/2¼ kg each), cut in half

3 tbsp salt

1 tbsp black pepper

1 tsp butter

6 whole fresh figs, quartered (see note)

1 cup demi-glace (see note)

Seared Beef Tenderloin with Red Wine & Peppercorn Jus

....

This is one of Jean-Francis's favorite dishes; you'll often see him sitting at the bar at one of our restaurants enjoying it, cooked blue-rare, of course! It was one of the initial recipes he created for our first Provence restaurant and has become a favorite for many of our customers as well. Serve with sautéed green beans. —A.

TO PREPARE OVEN-DRIED TOMATOES: Preheat oven to 325°F (165°C). Place tomatoes cut-side up on a baking sheet. Drizzle with oil and sprinkle with herbes de Provence and salt. Bake for 35–40 minutes, until tomatoes are wrinkled but slightly retaining their juices. Remove from oven and set aside.

Preheat oven to 475°F (250°C). Season steaks with pepper and 1 tsp salt. In an oven-safe frying pan on high, heat oil and 2 tbsp butter. (If you don't have an oven-safe frying pan, use a regular frying pan, then transfer steaks to a roasting pan for oven.) Once butter starts to brown, add steaks and thyme and sear for about 2 minutes on each side, until browned. Place pan with steaks directly into oven (or transfer to a roasting pan) for 3 minutes, then remove from oven, flip steaks, and return to oven for another 2 minutes. Remove from oven and transfer steaks to a cutting board to rest. Remove any excess oil from frying pan and return it to stove element

(continued)

OVEN-DRIED TOMATOES:

4 Roma tomatoes, halved lengthwise

2 tbsp olive oil

1 tsp herbes de Provence (see note on page 27)

1 tsp salt

4 steaks (6-oz/ 170-g each) beef tenderloin

½ tsp black pepper

1½ tsp salt

2 tbsp olive oil

3 tbsp butter

1 sprig thyme

1 cup red wine

1 cup demi-glace (see note)

½ tsp cracked black peppercorns

on high heat. Add wine and stir continually to deglaze pan, scraping the bottom and letting wine reduce until there is about 3 tbsp left. Add demi-glace and remaining ½ tsp salt and stir continually while liquid reduces for another 2 minutes; the sauce should be slightly thickened. Stir in pepper and remaining 1 tbsp butter. Place steaks onto individual plates and ladle sauce overtop; serve with oven-dried tomatoes.

MAKES 4 SERVINGS.

DEMI-GLACE IS A TRADITIONAL FRENCH BROWN SAUCE MADE WITH BEEF OR VEAL STOCK, SHERRY, AND ESPAGNOLE SAUCE. FOR HOME COOKS, IT'S EASIER TO PURCHASE IT; IT CAN BE FOUND AT ANY SPECIALTY MARKET. IT MAY BE SUBSTITUTED WITH ORGANIC BEEF STOCK.

Dijon-Roasted Chicken

....

This is a quick, easy, and delicious recipe you can prepare when you're in a hurry to get dinner on the table. Serve with roasted potatoes and a simple tossed salad.

In a large frying pan on high, heat butter and oil. Add chicken pieces and sear for 5 minutes on each side, until golden brown (use extra oil if necessary). Reduce heat to medium and add salt, pepper, garlic, bay leaves, thyme, and onions, and sauté for 3–4 minutes, until onions are lightly golden. Deglaze with wine, stirring continually for 3 minutes, allowing liquid to reduce slightly. Add mustard and demi-glace and stir to combine. Cover with lid, and simmer for about 40 minutes, turning chicken occasionally to cook evenly. To serve, remove chicken breasts first and place in center of a platter, then place remaining pieces of chicken around breasts. Strain sauce into a serving bowl, check seasoning and mustard flavors and adjust sauce as desired. Pour sauce over chicken or serve on the side.

Makes 4 servings.

Cutting up chicken is quite easy, but alternatively you can ask your butcher to do it for you.

Demi-glace is a traditional French brown sauce made with beef or veal stock, sherry, and espagnole sauce. For home cooks, it's easier to purchase it; it can be found at any specialty market. It may be substituted with organic beef stock.

2 tbsp butter

2 tbsp olive oil

2 small chickens, cut into 8 pieces each (see note)

1 tbsp salt

1 tbsp black pepper

10 cloves garlic

4 bay leaves

1 sprig fresh thyme

1 small red onion, sliced

2 cups white wine (for deglazing)

4–5 tbsp Dijon mustard

2 cups demi-glace (see note)

Roast Chicken with Herbes de Provence

....

2 whole chickens (about 4 lb/2 kg each), cut in half

2 tbsp herbes de Provence (see note on page 27)

2 tbsp salt

2 tbsp olive oil

Juice of ½ lemon

1 cup demi-glace (see note)

½ cup mixed fresh herbs (e.g., parsley, chives, basil)

There is nothing like a succulent roast chicken. The trick to keeping it moist is to cook it on the bone (cutting the chicken in half will help reduce cooking time while retaining moisture). There are also many fancy chicken rubs on the market but we think that herbes de Provence is all you really need.

Preheat oven to 475°F (250°C). In a large roasting pan, place chicken halves bone-side down. Sprinkle with herbes de Provence and salt and drizzle oil to coat evenly. Roast for 40 minutes, until chicken is golden brown and skin is crispy. Remove chicken from pan and place on a serving platter. Place pan on stove element on high heat and deglaze with lemon juice. Add demi-glace and stir continually for 1 minute, letting sauce reduce. Turn off heat, add fresh herbs, stir, and serve alongside chicken.

Makes 4–6 servings.

Demi-glace is a traditional French brown sauce made with beef or veal stock, sherry, and espagnole sauce. For home cooks, it's easier to purchase it; it can be found at any specialty market. It may be substituted with organic beef stock.

GRILLED QUAIL WITH JUNIPER BERRY JUS

....

I have fond memories of this dish, which is one of my mother's specialties. She often talks about the time I was a child and went through the garbage looking for leftover meat on the quail bones to eat. My tradition of savoring every last morsel has continued in our family; however, now I don't have to go through the garbage! During the summer months, take advantage of your barbecue to grill the quails instead of roasting them in the oven. Serve with Roasted Sweet Potatoes (page 103) and vegetables. —JF.

In a large frying pan on high heat, combine butter, onions, garlic, and juniper berries and sauté for 3–4 minutes to sweat onions, reducing heat slightly if necessary. Add wine and stir continually, allowing liquid to reduce by half. Reduce heat to low, add veal stock or beef bouillon, and stir to combine. Cover with lid and simmer for 10–15 minutes. Meanwhile, preheat oven to 400°F (205°C). Rub each quail with herbes de Provence. In a frying pan on high, heat oil. Add quails in batches and sear for 3–5 minutes on each side until browned (use extra oil if necessary), then place in roasting pan. Roast in oven for about 10 minutes, until golden brown. Remove from oven and place quails on a serving platter. Taste test jus, and season with salt if desired. Pour jus over quails and serve.

MAKES 4 SERVINGS (2 QUAILS PER SERVING).

QUAILS ARE SMALL AND GENERALLY DO NOT VARY IN SIZE. THEY ARE AVAILABLE FROM MOST GOURMET BUTCHERS. YOU MAY USE DE-BONED QUAIL IN THIS RECIPE; IF YOU DO, ROAST THEM IN THE OVEN FOR 4 MINUTES (AS OPPOSED TO 10 MINUTES FOR WHOLE QUAIL).

2 tbsp butter

½ white onion, sliced

1 tbsp garlic, chopped

1 tsp dried juniper berries, slightly crushed

1½ cup red wine

2 cups veal stock or beef bouillon

8 quails (see note)

1 tsp herbes de Provence (see note on page 27)

¼ cup olive oil

WHOLE BARBECUED RABBIT

....

Rabbit is choice meat for a summer barbecue. For those unfamiliar with it, rest assured it is really quite simple to prepare, and the result is a refreshing change from chicken. This recipe will surely transport you to the South of France!

2 whole rabbits, cut in half (see note)

2 tbsp garlic, minced

2 tbsp herbes de Provence (see note on page 27)

2 tbsp Dijon mustard

1 tbsp salt

1 tsp black pepper

2 tbsp canola oil

In a large baking dish, place rabbit halves. In a bowl, combine remaining ingredients, except oil, and pour over rabbit to coat evenly. Cover and refrigerate for about 1 hour to marinate. Preheat barbecue to medium heat and remove any sediment from grill. (If a barbecue is not available, you can use an oven; see note.) Coat grill with oil, then set rabbit meat-side down onto grill. Cook for 30–35 minutes, turning every 5 minutes until golden brown; it is important that the rabbit does not burn.

MAKES 4–6 SERVINGS.

RABBIT IS AVAILABLE FROM MOST GOURMET BUTCHERS. ASK YOUR BUTCHER TO CUT IT FOR YOU.

IF USING AN OVEN, PREHEAT TO 400ºF (205ºC). DRIZZLE 2 TBSP CANOLA OIL INTO ROASTING PAN, THEN PLACE MARINATED RABBIT BONE-SIDE DOWN INTO PAN AND ROAST FOR 30–40 MINUTES, UNTIL GOLDEN BROWN.

MATISSE'S FAVORITE RABBIT STEW WITH BABY CARROTS & BACON

¼ cup olive oil

2½ lb (1¼ kg) rabbit legs (see note)

1 tbsp salt

½ tbsp black pepper

1 medium onion, diced

5 cloves garlic, peeled

½ cup uncooked bacon, diced

1 cup button mushrooms, quartered

1 cup white wine

1 sprig fresh sage

2 bay leaves

4 cups water (more or less as needed)

16 baby carrots, peeled

Our son Matisse loves this stew. Rabbit has the texture of chicken but with a slightly "gamier" taste.

In a large pot on high, heat oil. Add rabbit, season with salt and pepper, and sear for about 1 minute on each side, until browned. Reduce heat to medium, add onions, garlic, bacon, and mushrooms, and sauté for about 4 minutes, until onions are translucent. Add wine, stir to combine, and cook for another 2 minutes. Stir in sage, bay leaves and enough water for it to come about ¾ up the way of rabbit. Cover with lid and simmer for 75–90 minutes, turning rabbit every 30 minutes to cook evenly. Add carrots, stir to combine, and continue to cook, uncovered, for another 15 minutes, stirring occasionally.

MAKES 4 SERVINGS.

RABBIT IS AVAILABLE FROM MOST GOURMET BUTCHERS. IF YOU CAN'T FIND RABBIT LEGS, FEEL FREE TO USE A WHOLE RABBIT CUT UP INTO 6 PIECES. ASK YOUR BUTCHER TO CUT IT FOR YOU.

Mamie Suzanne's Pork Pot Roast

....

We've eaten this dish of Mamie Suzanne for years but never quite understood how she created such an intensely flavored jus. Finally, we carefully watched her prepare it one day, and to our surprise it was easy; letting the liquid reduce creates a gelatinous sauce that's enhanced by the flavors of the meat. —A.

Cut 4 little slits in pork roast and insert 1 half-clove of garlic in each. In a large pot on high, heat oil. Add remaining garlic and onion and sauté for 3–4 minutes, until onions are translucent, reducing heat slightly if necessary. Add roast and sear for 2 minutes on each side, until browned. Add salt, pepper, thyme, and enough water to completely cover roast. Reduce heat and bring to a simmer, uncovered, for 3½ hours, until liquid is almost completely evaporated; there should be a golden brown sauce left in the bottom of the pot. Remove roast and let cool slightly before slicing. Serve jus alongside pork.

Makes 4 servings.

1 (2½-lb/1¼-kg) pork shoulder roast

6 cloves garlic, halved lengthwise

¼ medium onion, diced

2 tbsp olive oil

1 tbsp salt

1 tbsp black pepper

1 sprig thyme

5 cups water (more or less as needed)

Fragrant Curried Pork

....

1 (2½-lb/1¼-kg) pork shoulder roast or pork leg pieces, cut into large cubes

1 tbsp salt

1 tbsp black pepper

2 tbsp curry powder

½ cup + 2 tbsp canola oil

1 tbsp flour

½ medium onion, diced

3 tbsp garlic, chopped

2 tbsp fresh ginger, minced

¼ cup white wine

3 cups + 1 tbsp (750 mL) chicken stock (more or less as needed)

½ large red bell pepper, chopped

½ yellow or orange bell pepper, chopped

½ cup green onion, sliced (for garnish)

We admit that we're chefs who like to cook à la minute *(at the last minute), keeping it simple and not using too many ingredients. But when Mamie Suzanne comes to visit, she's always busy in our kitchen at home cooking 2 or 3 meals at a time, even in the early morning hours, filling our house with wonderful aromas that awaken our senses. This is one of those dishes that Mamie would be cooking; the kids and I love it, as the meat just melts in our mouths. Serve with steamed basmati rice.* —A.

In a stainless steel bowl, combine pork, salt, pepper, and curry powder and mix to coat meat evenly. In a frying pan on high, heat ¼ cup oil. Add half the pork and sear for about 2 minutes in each side, until all sides are browned. Sprinkle ½ tbsp flour to coat meat and stir to combine. Transfer meat to a large pot and set aside. Repeat process with remaining meat and flour. In the same frying pan on medium-high, heat remaining 2 tbsp oil. Add onions, garlic, and ginger and sauté for 3–4 minutes, until onions are translucent. Add wine and stir continually, letting liquid reduce by half, then transfer mixture into pot with the seared pork. Add enough chicken stock to completely cover pork, cover with lid, reduce heat to low, and bring to a simmer for 1½ hours. Add bell peppers, stir, and let simmer uncovered for another 30 minutes. Serve, sprinkled with green onions.

Makes 6 servings.

Involtini di Vitello (Italian Veal Stuffed with Spinach & Mozzarella)

And now for something non-French: Alessandra's dad often made this dish at Christmas or Easter time. It's a typical Italian dish that's great to serve on a big platter family-style with fresh pasta of your choice. This recipe requires 8 strong wooden toothpicks for the rolls. —JF.

Preheat oven to 400°F (205°C). On a clean work surface, lay veal cutlets lengthwise away from you. Season both sides of veal with a pinch of salt and pepper. Spread spinach on each piece of meat, distributing evenly. Sprinkle cheese evenly on spinach. Carefully roll up into small rolls, much like you would roll up a burrito, and secure each with a toothpick. In a large frying pan on high, heat butter and oil. Sear each roll for 2–3 minutes on each side until golden brown, then place, seam-side down, into a baking dish. Bake in oven for 10–15 minutes. Meanwhile, deglaze frying pan with wine and let reduce on high heat for 4–5 minutes. Add onion, garlic, and mushrooms and sauté for 2 minutes. Add stock and stir continually for another 4–5 minutes, allowing liquid to reduce. Taste test, and season with remaining salt and pepper if desired. Remove from heat, stir in parsley, pour over veal, and serve.

Makes 4–6 servings.

8 veal cutlets, pounded thin

Salt to taste

Freshly ground black pepper to taste

2 bunches spinach, slightly cooked and drained of excess water

1 lb (900 g) mozzarella cheese, grated

1 tbsp butter

2 tbsp olive oil

1 cup white wine (or cooking sherry)

½ medium onion, chopped

2 cloves garlic, minced

½ lb (225 g) mushrooms (e.g., button, cremini, chanterelles)

½ cup chicken stock

2 tbsp flat-leaf Italian parsley, chopped

Braised Lamb Shanks with Tomato Sauce

....

2 tbsp canola oil

4 lamb shanks (see note)

1 tbsp salt

1 tbsp black pepper

6 cloves garlic

2 cups white wine

2 cups lamb stock or veal stock (see note)

2 cans (13½-oz/400-mL each) plum tomatoes, whole or crushed (including juice)

2 bay leaves

1 tbsp whole black peppercorns

This recipe really warms the heart and stomach on a cold winter day. It's fairly easy to put together, although it does require a little extra lovin' to ensure the meat is cooked evenly. Serve with Soft Parmesan Polenta (page 108).

Preheat oven to 300°F (150°C). In a large frying pan on high, heat oil. Add shanks, sprinkle with salt and pepper, add garlic, and sear lamb for 2–3 minutes on each side until golden brown. Transfer shanks and garlic to a roasting pan. Deglaze frying pan with wine, scraping the bottom, then pour over shanks. Add lamb or veal stock, tomatoes (including juice), bay leaves, and peppercorns. Cover with lid and roast for about 2½–3 hours, turning lamb every 30 minutes to cook evenly; meat should be almost falling off the bone when ready.

Makes 4 servings.

Lamb shanks are often available fresh from your butcher, or frozen at most grocery stores.

Lamb or veal stock is available at most gourmet food stores.

RACK OF LAMB WITH DIJON-HERB CRUST

....

This is a popular dish at both of our restaurants, and it's frequently requested whenever we cook for guests at home. The combination of the fresh herbs and a Dijon crust is wonderful with the lamb. Serve with roasted vegetables.

In a large dish or platter, place lamb and drizzle with 1 tsp oil, and sprinkle with garlic and herbs de Provence. Cover and refrigerate for 1–2 hours to marinate. Preheat oven to 400°F (205°C). In a large sauté pan on high, heat remaining 1 tbsp + 2 tsp oil. Add lamb, season with salt and pepper, and sear for about 3 minutes on each side. Transfer to a roasting pan and roast in oven for 10–12 minutes, turning lamb over after 6 minutes. (This is the cooking time for medium-cooked lamb. If you prefer well done, roast for another 5 minutes more; or for medium rare, roast for 5 minutes less.) Remove from oven and transfer lamb to a plate to rest for about 10 minutes (see note). Do not turn off oven.

In a food processor, combine all topping ingredients and blend for about 3 minutes until completely incorporated and bright green in color.

Return lamb to roasting pan, spread mustard evenly on top of lamb and sprinkle with topping. Place in oven to quickly brown coating for another 2–3 minutes. Remove from oven, slice, and serve on a large platter.

MAKES 4–6 SERVINGS.

IT IS IMPORTANT THAT THE LAMB RESTS AFTER COOKING SO IT STAYS TENDER AND JUICY. THE GENERAL RULE OF THUMB IS THAT COOKED MEAT SHOULD IDEALLY REST FOR THE SAME AMOUNT OF TIME THAT IT WAS IN THE OVEN.

2 whole racks of lamb, cleaned and trimmed by butcher

2 tbsp olive oil

1 tsp garlic, chopped

1 tsp herbes de Provence (see note on page 27)

1 tsp salt

½ tsp black pepper

TOPPING:

1 cup breadcrumbs

1 tsp garlic, chopped

1 tbsp olive oil

1 cup fresh parsley

1 cup fresh basil leaves

2 tbsp Dijon mustard

LEG OF LAMB STUFFED WITH OLIVE TAPENADE

1 leg of lamb (about
6 lb/2¾ kg), deboned
by butcher

1 batch Tapenade
(page 73)

4 tbsp olive oil

1 tbsp salt

1 tbsp black pepper

1 tsp herbes de Provence
(see note on page 27)

8 cloves garlic (peel
3 cloves)

1 tbsp butter

3 sprigs fresh rosemary
(optional)

We like to make this recipe for last-minute gatherings. It's simple to prepare but makes a big impression! The key to keeping the meat tender is to allow it to rest long enough for the juice to be re-absorbed. Serve with Soft Parmesan Polenta (page 108) or Mushroom & Pearl Barley Risotto with Truffle Oil (page 105).

Preheat oven to 450°F (230°C). On a clean work surface, place lamb and spread tapenade in space where thigh bone has been removed. Close up space and tie with butcher string to contain tapenade. Cover lamb with 2 tbsp oil to coat evenly. Place in a shallow roasting pan, season with salt and pepper, and sprinkle herbes de Provence over top. Make 3 small incisions in meat and insert a peeled garlic clove in each. Drizzle lamb with remaining 2 tbsp oil and place butter in pan. Scatter remaining unpeeled garlic cloves and rosemary around lamb. Bake uncovered for 20 minutes. Then, reduce heat to 400°F (205°C) and roast for another 50–60 minutes for medium-rare. The internal temperature should be 145°F (65°C); test with a meat thermometer. Turn off oven and allow meat to rest for 10–15 minutes (see note). Remove lamb from oven and transfer to a cutting board, reserving garlic and juices from pan. Remove strings and slice some but not all lamb, cutting across leg so each slice has tapenade in center. Place uncarved section of leg at one end of a large serving platter and arrange slices, overlapping. Pour reserved garlic and juices from pan over lamb slices and serve.

MAKES 6–8 SERVINGS.

IT IS IMPORTANT THAT THE LAMB RESTS AFTER COOKING SO IT STAYS TENDER AND JUICY.

Ragoût d'Agneau

If it's not apparent already, we love lamb! Here is another variation of this very flavorful meat, which translates as Lamb Stew with White Beans. It's made with white wine, making the dish a bit lighter-tasting, so it's suitable to serve both in summer as well as winter.

In a large bowl, combine lamb, onions, carrots, celery, garlic, wine, and pepper and mix to combine. Cover and refrigerate overnight to marinate. The next day, strain liquid into a bowl and set aside (do not throw away). Separate meat from vegetables. In a large pot on high, heat oil. Sauté lamb for 2–3 minutes, in batches if necessary, until browned on all sides. Add reserved liquid and bring to a boil. Once boiling, reduce heat to medium, add reserved vegetables and thyme, and stir to combine. Cover with lid and simmer for 1½ hours, stirring occasionally. Add beans, stir to combine, and simmer for another 5–10 minutes, stirring occasionally; when ready, meat should be tender and vegetables should be very soft and incorporated into the stew.

MAKES 6 SERVINGS.

CANNELLINI (WHITE KIDNEY) BEANS ARE GOOD FOR THIS RECIPE.

2½ lb (1 kg) boneless lamb shoulder, cut into 2-in (5-cm) cubes (see note)

1 medium onion, chopped

1 carrot, chopped

2 celery stalks, chopped

5 cloves garlic

3 cups + 1 tbsp (750 mL) white wine

1 tbsp black pepper

½ cup olive oil

2 sprigs thyme

1 can (13½-oz/398-mL) white beans, drained and rinsed (see note)

Lamb Sirloin with Curried Israeli Couscous

....

LAMB:

4 steaks (6-oz/170-g each) lamb sirloin

1 tbsp herbes de Provence (see note on page 27)

1 tsp garlic purée

2 tbsp olive oil

1 tbsp salt

2 cups Lamb Jus, heated (see opposite page)

4 thick slices Spanish onion

1 tbsp extra virgin olive oil (for onion)

COUSCOUS:

4 qt (4 L) water

1 tsp curry powder

1¼ tsp salt

2 cups dry Israeli couscous (see note)

2 tbsp olive oil

½ tsp butter

8 cups fresh spinach, chopped

1 medium tomato, diced

If you love rack of lamb but don't love its expensive price tag, this is a great alternative. The sirloins remain still very tender when cooked to medium rare or medium (but not beyond that). To save prep time, prepare the jus in advance, and marinate the lamb the night before.

TO PREPARE LAMB: Place steaks in a large baking dish. In a bowl, mix herbes de Provence, garlic, and 1 tbsp oil, then pour over lamb to coat evenly. Cover and refrigerate for 2 hours or overnight to marinate. Preheat oven to 400°F (205°C). In a large frying pan on high, heat remaining 1 tbsp oil. Add marinated lamb, season with salt, and sear for about 2–3 minutes on each side, until browned all over. Transfer to a roasting pan and place in oven to roast, 8–12 minutes for medium rare, 12–16 minutes for medium (do not cook past medium); flip lamb once halfway through cooking time. Remove from oven and allow to rest (see note).

Reduce oven temperature to 350°F (180°C). Rub each slice of onion with oil. If using a barbecue or stovetop grill, on high heat, grill onion for 2 minutes on each side; or if using a frying pan, on high heat, sear onions for 2 minutes on each side. Place onions on baking sheet and bake for 8–10 minutes.

TO PREPARE COUSCOUS: Meanwhile, in a large pot on high heat, combine water, curry powder, and 1 tsp salt. Bring to a boil, add couscous, and cook as you would pasta, for 8–10 minutes until al dente. Strain couscous, then transfer to a large bowl and drizzle with 2 tbsp oil and toss so it does not stick. In a frying pan on medium heat, melt butter. Add spinach and remaining ¼ tsp salt and sauté for 3–4 minutes, until spinach is wilted. Strain all excess water. Add spinach to couscous, then tomatoes, and mix to combine. Check for seasoning.

To serve, place couscous mixture in middle of each plate. Slice lamb and place beside couscous; top with onion slice and drizzle with lamb jus. Reserve some jus to serve on the side.

Makes 4 servings.

Israeli couscous, also known as pearl couscous, is slightly larger than the popular North African variation and cooked al dente, like pasta.

It is important that the lamb rests after cooking so it stays tender and juicy. The general rule of thumb is that cooked meat should rest for the same amount of time that was in the oven.

Lamb Jus

This jus can be made in up to 3 days in advance, and stored in the freezer for up to 3 months. Makes 3 cups.

2 lb (900 g) lamb bones

3 qt (3 L) water

1 carrot, chopped

1 medium onion, chopped

2 celery stalks, chopped

Preheat oven to 450°F (230°C). Place bones on a roasting sheet and roast for 2 hours, flipping once halfway after 1 hour, until bones are evenly dark brown. In a large pot on high heat, combine water, carrots, onions, celery, and bones and bring to a boil. Once boiling, reduce heat to low, cover with lid, and simmer for 4 hours. Strain liquid through a sieve into a pot, discarding bones and vegetables. Return to medium heat and let stock reduce to 3 cups, about 30 minutes, stirring frequently. Use immediately, or let cool completely before storing in refrigerator or freezer.

Brunch

Croque Monsieur Eggs Benedict

Baby Shrimp Eggs Benedict

Crabcake Eggs Benedict

Crab & Lobster Omelette

Smoked Salmon Omelette

Alessandra's Sunday Quiche

Chicken Crêpes

Remi & Matisse's Crêpes

Provence-Style French Toast

Jam-Filled Brioche

Healthy Banana Muffins

Currant & Flax Scones

Clarified Butter

CROQUE MONSIEUR EGGS BENEDICT

....

Croque Monsieur is a classic hot sandwich made with ham and melted Gruyère cheese, served in most cafés and bakeries in France. In this recipe, we've taken tradition and turned it into a delicious breakfast treat. Serve with sautéed baby potatoes and fresh fruit of your choice.

TO PREPARE SUN-DRIED TOMATO BUTTER: Reconstitute sun-dried tomatoes in hot water, then drain. In a blender or food processor on medium, add sun-dried tomatoes and pulse until almost puréed. Transfer to a bowl, add butter, and mix until just combined, then set aside.

Preheat oven to 450°F (230°C). In a large saucepan on high heat, bring water and vinegar to a boil, then reduce heat to simmer. With a bread knife, slice focaccia square in half to be open-faced, then slice each diagonally to make 4 triangles total. On each focaccia triangle, spread a thin layer of sun-dried tomato butter, then top with ham, then cheese, distributed evenly. Place on a baking sheet and bake for 4 minutes. Meanwhile, crack 1 egg into small bowl, then gently drop into simmering water. Repeat with rest of eggs, a few at a time. Poach for about 3 minutes for a medium poach. With a slotted spoon, carefully remove eggs and transfer to a dry towel to soak up excess water. Remove focaccia from oven and place each triangle onto a plate, top each with 2 poached eggs and ¼ cup Hollandaise.

MAKES 4 SERVINGS.

SUN-DRIED TOMATO BUTTER:

2 slices sun-dried tomatoes (dried, not oil-packed)

½ cup hot water

4 tbsp butter, softened

1 gal (4 L) water

1 cup white vinegar

6×6-in (15×15-cm) square of focaccia

4 oz (115 g) Black Forest ham, sliced

4 oz (115 g) Gruyère cheese, grated

8 eggs

1 cup Hollandaise Sauce (page 84) (prepared immediately before making eggs)

Baby Shrimp Eggs Benedict

....

1 gal (4 L) water

1 cup white vinegar

8 whole eggs

1 cup precooked hand-peeled fresh baby shrimp (may use frozen)

1 tsp garlic, chopped

1 tbsp clarified butter (page 182)

1 tbsp fresh parsley, chopped

2 croissants

1 cup Hollandaise Sauce (page 84) (prepared immediately before making eggs)

½ medium lemon, cut in wedges

¼ tsp salt

⅛ tsp black pepper

This is a new twist on an old favorite—using a croissant instead of an English muffin for the base gives it a French touch! Serve with sautéed potatoes and fresh fruit.

In a large saucepan on high heat, bring water and vinegar to a boil, then reduce heat to simmer. Crack 1 egg into a small bowl, then gently drop into same pot of simmering water. Repeat with rest of eggs, a few at a time. Poach eggs for 3 minutes for a medium poach. While eggs cook, in a bowl, combine shrimp, garlic, 1 tbsp clarified butter, and parsley and mix together. Slice each croissant lengthwise and place each half on a plate. With a slotted spoon, carefully remove eggs and transfer to a clean towel to soak up excess water. Divide shrimp mixture evenly onto each croissant and top with 2 poached eggs and Hollandaise. Squeeze lemon over each and season with salt and pepper.

Makes 4 servings.

CRABCAKE EGGS BENEDICT

....

This recipe is time-consuming if you include preparation of the crabcakes and Hollandaise sauce, but it's worth every minute. Invite some friends over to help and have a few laughs while you cook. Serve with sautéed baby potatoes and fresh fruit of your choice.

In a large saucepan on high heat, bring water and vinegar to a boil, then reduce heat to simmer. In a frying pan on high, heat oil. Add crabcakes and sear on each side, then remove from heat and set aside. Crack 1 egg into a small bowl, then add to simmering water. Repeat with rest of eggs, a few at a time. Poach eggs for about 3 minutes for medium. With a slotted spoon, carefully remove eggs and place on a dry towel to soak up excess water. To assemble, place 2 crabcakes on each plate. Top each with 1 poached egg, then ¼ cup Hollandaise.

MAKES 4 SERVINGS.

1 gal (4 L) water

1 cup white vinegar

2 tbsp canola or olive oil

8 Crabcakes (page 53)

10 eggs

1 cup Hollandaise Sauce (page 84) (prepared immediately before making eggs)

CRAB & LOBSTER OMELETTE

....

This is a delicious indulgence for a sunny Sunday morning that will bring a little Provence into your home. Pre-cook the lobster and crab the day before to avoid the extra work in the morning. Serve with sautéed potatoes and fresh fruit of your choice.

12 eggs

1 pinch salt

1 pinch black pepper

¼ cup clarified butter (page 182)

4 oz (115 g) crab meat, cooked

4 oz (115 g) lobster meat, cooked

2 tbsp fresh mixed herbs (e.g., parsley, chives, basil)

In a large mixing bowl, whisk eggs with salt and pepper. In a large non-stick frying pan on medium-high heat, melt clarified butter. Add eggs and stir continuously with a rubber spatula. When eggs begin to coagulate, add crab and lobster, gently moving it to allow eggs to settle on the bottom of the pan (see note). Remove pan from heat. Sprinkle with herbs, then with a wide spatula, fold omelette over gently. Gently transfer omelette to a platter and serve.

MAKES 4 SERVINGS.

A TRUE FRENCH OMELETTE IS PLAIN-LOOKING; THE ONLY COLOR IS THAT OF THE EGGS, NOT REVEALING ITS DELICIOUS FILLING OR DISPLAYING ANY BROWN MARKS FROM THE PAN.

SMOKED SALMON OMELETTE

....

12 eggs

½ tsp salt

½ tsp pepper

1 small bunch of fresh chives, minced

¼ cup clarified butter (page 182)

4 slices smoked salmon

4 tsp cream cheese, softened

This is another delicious variation of the classic omelette. Serve with sautéed potatoes and fresh fruit.

In a large bowl, whisk eggs. Add salt, pepper, and chives, and stir to combine. In a large non-stick frying pan on medium-high, heat clarified butter. Add eggs and stir gently but continuously with a rubber spatula (do not scramble). When eggs begin to coagulate, allow them to settle at the bottom of pan and gently add salmon and cream cheese (see note). Once the surface of the eggs is cooked, with a wide spatula, fold omelette over gently, then transfer to a platter and serve.

MAKES 4 SERVINGS.

A TRUE FRENCH OMELETTE IS PLAIN-LOOKING; THE ONLY COLOR IS THAT OF THE EGGS, NOT REVEALING ITS DELICIOUS FILLING OR DISPLAYING ANY BROWN MARKS FROM THE PAN.

ALESSANDRA'S SUNDAY QUICHE

....

Quiche is one of the most versatile recipes that can be prepared with many combinations of flavors. So go ahead and be imaginative if you want to experiment! See the Fresh Tomato Tarte recipe on page 48 to make the pastry dough.

Ensure pâte brisée dough has been refrigerated for 1 hour. In a sauté pan on medium, heat oil. Add onions and sauté for about 5 minutes, until they are golden brown, then set aside to cool. On a lightly floured surface, turn out dough and roll into a circle about ¼-in (1-cm) thick to form a quiche shell. Transfer shell to an 8-in (20-cm) pie pan, cover with plastic wrap, and chill in the refrigerator for an additional 20 minutes. Preheat oven to 325°F (160°C). In a large bowl, add whipping cream, eggs, salt, and pepper and mix until well combined, then set aside. Remove pastry shell from fridge and remove plastic wrap. Remove pastry shell from refrigerator, layer with ham, sautéed onions, spinach, and cheese, then pour egg mixture on top. Bake for 40 minutes, until surface is light golden brown. Remove from oven and allow to cool for 5 minutes before serving.

MAKES 4 SERVINGS.

PÂTE BRISÉE (MEANING BROKEN-TEXTURED PASTRY) IS A SIMPLE AND DELICIOUS SHORT-CRUST PASTRY SHELL. USE THE RECIPE ON PAGE 48.

1 pâte brisée (pastry dough) (see note)

¼ cup canola oil

1 medium onion, sliced

1 cup whipping cream

2 eggs

1 tsp salt

1 tsp black pepper

1 cup Black Forest ham, diced

2 cups spinach

1 cup Gruyère cheese, grated

CHICKEN CRÊPES

2 cups Velouté Sauce
(page 85)

12 crêpes (see note)

FILLING:

4 boneless, skinless
chicken breasts

5 tbsp olive oil

1 tsp herbes de Provence
(see note on page 27)

3 tsp salt

2 tbsp garlic, chopped

2 cups mixed mushrooms
(e.g., button, oyster,
shiitake), sliced

8 asparagus stalks, cut
into ½-in/1-cm pieces
(see note)

2 cups Gruyère cheese,
grated (for garnish)

Fresh mixed herbs
(e.g., parsley, basil,
chives) (for garnish)

This is one of our most popular brunch items and has been on our menu since the restaurant first opened. Chicken Crêpes are a great savory alternative for weekend mornings. Serve with sautéed potatoes and fresh fruit of your choice.

TO PREPARE FILLING: Season chicken breasts with 1 tbsp oil, herbes de Provence, and 1 tsp salt. Over a grill or stove, in a frying pan on high, sauté seasoned and oiled chicken on both sides for 8–10 minutes, until cooked, then remove from heat to cool. Cut chicken into cubes, place in bowl, and set aside. In a sauté pan on medium, heat another 2 tbsp oil. Add garlic, mushrooms, and another 1 tsp salt and sauté until tender, then transfer to a bowl and set aside. In the same sauté pan on medium, heat remaining 2 tbsp oil. Add asparagus and sauté for about 2 minutes until tender, then transfer to a separate bowl and set aside.

TO ASSEMBLE CRÊPES: In a saucepan on medium heat, bring Velouté Sauce to simmer. Add chicken, garlic and mushrooms, and asparagus, and stir to combine. While waiting for mixture to return to simmer, arrange 3 crêpes on each plate. Once mixture is simmering, spoon about ¼ cup onto half of each crêpe, then fold over and sprinkle with cheese and herbs. Repeat until all crêpes are filled.

MAKES 4 SERVINGS.

SEE PAGE 175 FOR THE RECIPE FOR CRÊPES; HOWEVER, OMIT THE SUGAR FOR MAKING THESE SAVORY CRÊPES.

USE LEFTOVER CRÊPES AS SNACKS THE NEXT DAY, SPREADING THEM WITH JAM OR NUTELLA.

SELECT ASPARAGUS THAT HAVE FIRM, CRISP STALKS OF EVEN THICKNESS, WITH TIGHTLY CLOSED TIPS. YOUNG ASPARAGUS NEEDS ONLY THE WOODY STEM SNAPPED OFF; HOWEVER, OLDER ASPARAGUS MAY ALSO NEED PEELING.

REMI & MATISSE'S CRÊPES

·····················

Matisse and Remi love crêpes! They used to drag us out of bed to make them on weekends. But one early Sunday morning after a late night at the restaurant, when Remi again wanted us to make crêpes, my husband pulled himself out of bed, took both boys downstairs, and showed them how to cook their own. What a pleasure it is to now wake up on Sunday mornings to crêpes made by our sons. Serve with maple syrup on the side and enjoy! —A.

1½ cups flour

1 tbsp sugar

1 tsp lemon or orange zest

3 cups milk

4 eggs

1 tbsp vanilla

¼ cup butter, melted

¼ cup clarified butter (to brush pan) (see note)

In a large bowl, combine flour, sugar, and zest in a bowl and mix together. In a separate bowl, combine the milk, eggs, and vanilla. Slowly add wet ingredients to dry and combine until just mixed (do not overmix). Add melted butter and fold until just mixed. Cover and set aside for 1 hour (or overnight). In a non-stick frying pan on medium heat, brush on some clarified butter. With a small ladle, drop ¼ cup batter onto pan and tilt to form a thin circular crêpe. When edges turn golden brown, flip to cook other side until golden brown. Remove from pan. Repeat until batter is all used; brush additional clarified butter on pan only when necessary.

MAKES 4 SERVINGS (ABOUT 15 CRÊPES).

SEE PAGE 182 ON HOW TO MAKE CLARIFIED BUTTER, OR YOU MAY SUBSTITUTE WITH VEGETABLE OIL.

YOU MAY WANT TO TRY OUR FAVORITE FILLINGS FOR CRÊPES: NUTELLA, FRESH FRUIT, OR FRESHLY SQUEEZED LEMON AND SUGAR.

Provence-Style French Toast

Although this is called "French" toast or pain perdue*, it is not a common breakfast dish in France. During the year that I lived in Marseille, I would crave it. Finally one day I decided to make French toast for the family, using a day-old baguette and maple syrup that my mom sent from Canada!* —A.

In a small pot on medium, gently heat berries to break them down, stirring continually. Stir in maple syrup when berries have evaporated ⅓ of their juice and set aside. With a bread knife, slice baguette diagonally into 1-in (2½-cm) thick slices. In a bowl, whisk together milk, eggs, and vanilla. On a plate, combine sugar and cinnamon. In a large frying pan on medium heat, heat clarified butter or oil. Gently soak 2–4 bread slices (depending on how many can fit in pan) in egg-milk mixture until bread is heavy with mixture. Fry soaked bread on each side for 2–3 minutes until golden brown. Remove bread and coat both sides with the sugar-cinnamon mixture. Repeat process until all bread is used. To serve, reheat topping if necessary, then spoon over French toast and serve whipped cream on the side.

MAKES 4 SERVINGS.

TOPPING:

1 cup mixed berries (frozen is fine when not in season)

½ cup maple syrup

1 day-old French baguette

1 cup milk

4 eggs

2 tsp vanilla

½ cup sugar

3 tbsp cinnamon

1 tbsp clarified butter (page 182) or canola oil

½ cup whipped cream (optional, but decadent!)

Jam-Filled Brioche

1 tsp dry active yeast

2 tbsp sugar

1 tsp vanilla extract

3 eggs

1⅔ cups flour

2 tbsp butter, diced into
1-in (2½-cm) cubes and
softened

½ cup raspberry jam

1 egg, whisked
(for finishing)

2 tbsp raw sugar
(for finishing)

The classic French brioche *is a bread that is rich with butter and eggs. This recipe takes some time to make but has always been a hit on our brunch menu. With a little patience and love, it will turn out great! Feel free to substitute with any jam you like. Note that you need to prepare the dough the day before.*

THE DAY BEFORE: In the bowl of a mixer with a paddle attachment, add yeast, sugar, and vanilla and mix on low speed for about 30 seconds, until ingredients are well combined. Add eggs while mixer is still on low speed, and continue to mix until eggs are incorporated. Turn mixer off, remove bowl from mixer and add flour. Return bowl to mixer and mix on low speed for about 1 minute, until just mixed. Reduce to lowest speed and slowly add butter. Continue to mix until batter is smooth and butter has been distributed throughout. Transfer dough to a separate bowl and cover with plastic wrap. Place in a warm area and let rise for about 4 hours, until it doubles in size. Chill in refrigerator overnight.

THE NEXT DAY: Remove dough from refrigerator. On a lightly floured surface, turn dough out and separate into 8 equal pieces that are the size of tennis balls. Slightly flatten dough and place 1 tbsp jam in center of each piece, then bring the opposite corners together and pinch them together to encase the jam. Repeat this process with other 2 corners. Each brioche should be ball-shaped. On a baking sheet lined with parchment paper, place brioche and leave on countertop to rest for 1 hour at room temperature.

Preheat oven to 350°F (180°C). Brush brioche tops with whisked egg and sprinkle with raw sugar. Bake for 25 minutes, until golden brown.

MAKES 8 SERVINGS.

INSTEAD OF JAM, TRY USING NUTELLA, OR SOME *DOLCE DE LECHE* (CARAMELIZED CONDENSED MILK) TO MAKE THE BRIOCHE EVEN MORE DECADENT!

Healthy Banana Muffins

½ cup sugar

½ cup brown sugar

½ cup butter

1 egg

1 cup ripe bananas, mashed

1 tsp baking soda

2 tbsp hot water

½ cup all purpose flour

½ cup whole wheat flour

½ cup flax meal

1 tbsp butter (to coat muffin pan)

1 tbsp flour (to dust muffin pan)

This recipe is so easy, quick, and delicious. I often make the mini-version of these muffins for our sons' school snacks. Apparently all their friends line up for a taste when they see them in Matisse and Remi's lunch boxes. —A.

Preheat oven to 350°F (180°C). In a bowl, cream together sugars and butter. Add egg and bananas and mix well. In a separate dish, dissolve baking soda in hot water, then add to banana mixture. In another bowl, combine flours and flax meal, then fold into banana mixture until just mixed (do not overmix). Butter muffin pan and dust with flour. Spoon batter evenly and bake for 12–15 minutes (for mini muffins) or about 25 minutes (for regular-sized muffins), until a toothpick inserted in center comes out clean.

MAKES 24 MINI MUFFINS OR 9 REGULAR-SIZED MUFFINS.

CURRANT & FLAX SCONES

....

An important step in making fluffy scones is to make sure you do not overmix the dough.

2½ cups whipping cream

2 cups all-purpose flour

½ cup whole wheat flour

1 tbsp baking powder

2 tbsp icing sugar

¼ cup dried currants

½ cup flax meal

2 tbsp milk

Preheat oven to 350°F (180°C). In a large bowl, whisk whipping cream until soft peaks form. Sift in flours, baking powder, and icing sugar and stir to combine. Add currants and flax meal and stir until just combined (do not overmix). Turn out dough onto a lightly floured surface and roll out into a square about 1-in (2½-cm) thick. Cut into 15 equal squares (re-rolling dough if necessary). Place scones on a baking pan and brush tops with milk. Bake for 12–15 minutes, until an inserted toothpick comes out clean.

MAKES 15 SCONES.

THESE SWEET SCONES CAN BE MADE SAVORY BY OMITTING SUGAR AND CURRANTS AND ADDING ¼ CUP GRUYÈRE CHEESE, 1 TSP HERBES DE PROVENCE (SEE NOTE ON PAGE 27), AND ½ TSP SALT TO THE BATTER.

CLARIFIED BUTTER

....

1 lb (450 g) butter (salted or unsalted), cut into 1-in (2½-cm) cubes

Clarified butter is widely used in our breakfast preparations. It can be tricky to make at first, but once you get the hang of it you'll find yourself using it more often for breakfast and other dishes. Clarified butter keeps longer than regular butter since the water has been removed. Once cooled, store in a sealed container in the refrigerator.

STOVETOP METHOD: In a medium-sized saucepan on medium heat, place butter. Once butter starts to melt, reduce heat to low. Stir continually to ensure it does not burn; it will start to bubble but will eventually subside. After about 5 minutes, the butter should look separated. When this occurs, remove from heat and let stand for 2 minutes. Skim off the solids that are floating on top of the clarified butter, and do not use the water that has accumulated at the bottom of the pan.

MICROWAVE METHOD: In a microwaveable dish (it is best to use a glass dish so you can watch over it), place butter. Microwave on medium-high for 10 minutes. Remove from microwave and let stand for 2 minutes. Skim off the solids that are floating on top of the clarified butter, and do not use the water that has accumulated at the bottom of the dish.

MAKES ¾–1 CUP.

Desserts

Pear & Fig Tarte

Pear Frangipane Tarte

Apple Tarte Tatin

Lemon Tarte

Hazelnut Brittle

Nectarine & Basil Crostada

Soupe aux Fruits Rouges
(Fresh Berry Soup)

Clafoutis with White Chocolate
& Mixed Berries

Torta di Capodanno

Raspberry Crème Brûlée

Peach & White Chocolate
Bread Pudding

Truffle Cake

Flambée Bananas

Moist Chocolate Layer Cake

Chocolate Espresso Pot de Crème

Tiramisu

Lavender & Orange Cheesecake with
Mixed Berry Compote

Pear & Fig Tarte

....

This is one of those desserts that I created on a whim one day when I had an abundance of figs and pears. Using puff pastry stored in the freezer, it turned out to be a real winner! —A.

1 sheet of puff pastry
(see notes)

4 pears, each peeled and
cut into 6 wedges

8 fresh figs, cut in half

½ cup unsalted butter

¼ cup sugar

Preheat oven to 375°F (190°C). On a baking sheet with parchment paper, place sheet of puff pastry. Arrange pear wedges on pastry in 4 rows of 6, top each row of pears with 4 fig halves. Dot rows with butter and sprinkle with sugar. Bake for 15–20 minutes until golden brown.

MAKES 6 SERVINGS.

FEEL FREE TO SUBSTITUTE THE PEARS AND/OR FIGS WITH ANY FRUIT IN SEASON.

THE SHEET OF PUFF PASTRY YOU USE SHOULD BE LARGE ENOUGH TO COVER THE BAKING SHEET.

PUFF PASTRY, WHICH IS CALLED *PÂTÉ FEUILLETÉE* IN FRANCE, IS SOLD FROZEN IN SHEETS AND IS AVAILABLE IN MOST GROCERY STORES. AFTER THAWING TO USE, KEEP IT COVERED WITH A MOIST TOWEL TO PREVENT IT FROM DRYING.

Pear Frangipane Tarte

....

ALMOND MIXTURE (to be prepared the night before):

1 cup butter

1 cup icing (confectioner's) sugar

2¼ cups ground almonds

⅓ cup flour

5 eggs, lightly beaten

PASTRY SHELL:

2 cups flour

¼ tsp salt

⅓ cup sugar

½ cup cold butter

1 egg

1 tbsp ice cold water

3 Bartlett pears, peeled, halved, and seeded

This is a great fall dessert when pears are in season! This recipe requires a 10–12-in (25–30-cm) tarte pan which, in contrast to a pie pan, has a removable bottom and straight sides.

TO PREPARE ALMOND MIXTURE: In a mixer on medium speed, beat butter until very soft. Add icing sugar, almonds, and flour and beat well. Add eggs, one by one, incorporating after each one. Transfer to a clean bowl, cover, and refrigerate for up to 24 hours.

TO PREPARE PASTRY SHELL: In a large bowl, combine flour, salt, and sugar and cut in butter until butter resembles small peas. Make a hole in center of mixture, add egg, and mix to combine. Slowly add ice cold water and mix until just combined (do not overmix), then roll into a ball. Cover in plastic wrap and refrigerate for at least 30 minutes. Remove from refrigerator and on a lightly floured surface, roll into a circle ¼-in (½-cm) thick and place into a 10- or 12-in (25- or 30-cm) tarte pan.

Preheat oven to 350°F (180°C). Pour almond mixture into pastry shell, then evenly distribute pears, flat-side down (see note). Bake for about 45 minutes, or until golden brown.

MAKES 10 SERVINGS.

DO NOT OVERFILL PASTRY SHELL WITH ALMOND MIXTURE, AS IT MAY OVERFLOW DURING BAKING. ANY LEFTOVER FILLING CAN BE USED FOR A SMALLER TARTE.

Apple Tarte Tatin

....

When making this dessert, Alessandra has to make an extra tart just for our kids because they love it as much as adults do. Serve with vanilla ice cream. This recipe requires a thick-bottomed, oven-safe, 10-in (25-cm) frying pan. —JF.

1½ cups sugar

½ cup water

8–10 Golden Delicious apples, peeled, cored, and cut in half or quarters

2 tbsp butter

1 tsp fresh ginger, grated (optional)

1 sheet puff pastry (see note)

Preheat oven to 350°F (180°C). In a thick-bottomed, oven-safe, 10-in (25-cm) frying pan on medium heat, melt sugar and water, but do not stir—allow mixture to come to a boil and gently tilt pan to distribute evenly (this way, caramelization will occur quickly). When sugar turns a rich cognac color, add apples and butter. The sugar will continue to caramelize but the addition of apples and butter will slow down this process. Reduce heat to medium-low, allowing apples to be covered with sugar. Add ginger. Turn apples with tongs or a fork every 3–5 minutes so they are well coated. Once apples become somewhat transparent, arrange them in a circle with some in the middle. With a spoon, remove excess juice from pan. Remove pan from heat and place puff pastry sheet over apples. Poke pastry with a fork then place pan in oven to bake for 10–12 minutes. Remove from oven and let cool for 5 minutes. Carefully turn pan over a large plate to release tarte and serve.

MAKES 6 SERVINGS.

PUFF PASTRY, WHICH IS CALLED *PÂTÉ FEUILLETÉE* IN FRANCE, IS SOLD FROZEN IN SHEETS AND IS AVAILABLE IN MOST GROCERY STORES. AFTER THAWING TO USE, KEEP IT COVERED WITH A MOIST TOWEL TO PREVENT IT FROM DRYING.

THIS RECIPE CAN ALSO BE PREPARED WITH PEARS, PINEAPPLES, AND ANY FRUIT WITH PITS. PEAR AND GINGER IS A DELICIOUS COMBINATION.

LEMON TARTE

·······················

Jean-Francis's mother Suzanne often brags about her son's ability to bake when he was only eight years old. Whenever she had guests over, Jean-Francis would take the initiative and bake a Lemon Tarte or Sacher Torte for which he soon became famous. Serve with Hazelnut Brittle (page 191), whipped cream, and fruit coulis (optional). This recipe will require a 10-in (25-cm) tarte pan which, in contrast to a pie pan, has a removable bottom and straight sides. —A.

TO PREPARE DOUGH: In a large bowl, combine flour, salt, and sugar and cut in butter until butter resembles small peas. Make a hole in center of mixture and add egg and mix until just combined. Slowly mix in water, then roll into a ball with your hands. Return dough to bowl, cover in plastic wrap, and refrigerate for at least 30 minutes. Preheat oven to 375°F (190°C). Lightly oil a 10-in (25-cm) tarte pan or line with parchment paper. Remove dough from refrigerator and roll out into a ¼-in (½-cm) thick circle and place in pan. Refrigerate again for 30 minutes (place dried beans or weights on top of dough to prevent shrinking). Remove dough from refrigerator, remove beans or weights, and par-bake for 15–20 minutes. Remove from oven and set aside.

(continued)

DOUGH:

2 cups flour

¼ tsp salt

⅓ cup sugar

⅓ lb (150 g) cold butter

1 egg

2 tbsp ice cold water

FILLING:

Zest from 3 lemons (zest lemons before juicing, see below)

Juice of 8–9 lemons (about 1 cup)

2½ cups cold water

6 eggs

¾ cup sugar

1 tsp vanilla extract

½ cup cornstarch

Hazelnut Brittle (for garnish) (page 191)

TO PREPARE FILLING: Preheat oven to 350°F (180°C). In a large pot on medium heat, combine filling ingredients and stir continually with a wooden spoon for 5–8 minutes. Once mixture thickens and starts to bubble, remove from heat and strain into a bowl (discard what remains in strainer). Let liquid in bowl stand for 2–3 minutes to cool slightly.

Pour filling in par-baked tarte shell. Finish baking for 10–15 minutes until golden brown. Remove and let cool uncovered, then place in refrigerator for 2–3 hours to set. Serve with Hazelnut Brittle sprinkled over cooled tarte.

MAKES 8 SERVINGS.

THIS RECIPE CAN ALSO BE USED TO MAKE 6 INDIVIDUAL TARTES.

Hazelnut Brittle

....

We added this recipe to the menu after we opened our first Provence, using it as a garnish for the Lemon Tarte (page 189; see page 188 for photo), which consequently turned it into our signature dessert.

1 cup sugar

¾ cup toasted hazelnuts, chopped

In a medium saucepan on medium heat, add sugar. Stir continually while sugar caramelizes for about 5 minutes, or until it turns a cognac-brown color. Remove from heat and stir in hazelnuts. On a baking sheet lined with parchment paper, transfer mixture, pat down, and let cool for about 2 hours. Break into small pieces and serve.

Makes 1 cup.

The finished brittle can also be put through a food processor to create a fine caramel dust to sprinkle over any dessert.

Nectarine & Basil Crostada

....

PASTRY SHELL:

4 cups flour

½ cup sugar

½ cup cornmeal

1 lb (450 g) unsalted butter, cut into 1-in (2½-cm) cubes

3 eggs

2 tbsp water

FILLING:

3 lb (1½ kg) nectarines, pitted and quartered

½ cup sugar

1 tsp cornstarch

12 leaves of basil

1 egg mixed with 1 tbsp water (for egg wash)

Sugar (for finishing)

This fruit pie is an ideal dessert in the summer months when nectarines are at their best. You can substitute nectarines with any combination of fruit in this recipe, but we feel this one perfectly represents a beautiful day in the South of France. Serve with French vanilla ice cream. This recipe requires a 12-in (30-cm) pie pan.

TO PREPARE PASTRY SHELL: In a mixer on low speed, combine flour, sugar, and cornmeal. Add butter and continue to mix until butter resembles small peas. Add 3 eggs and water and mix until just combined (do not overmix). On a lightly floured surface, turn dough out. Divide dough in half and roll out one half into a circle ¼-in (½-cm) thick and place in 12-in (30-cm) pie pan. Roll out remaining dough to ⅛-in (5-mm) thickness, then cut into strips for a lattice top and set aside.

TO PREPARE FILLING: In a pot on medium-low heat, combine nectarines, sugar, and cornstarch and cook for 5–8 minutes, stirring continually. Add basil and stir to combine.

Preheat oven to 350°F (180°C). Pour fruit mixture into pie shell and criss-cross with strips of dough over top. Brush with egg wash and sprinkle with sugar. Bake for about 75 minutes, or until golden brown.

MAKES 10 SERVINGS.

Soupe aux Fruits Rouges (Fresh Berry Soup)

This is one of our favorite desserts on a hot summer day. It is easy to make and very refreshing. We have to give credit to my mother, Suzanne, for this recipe, which used to be a signature dessert at her restaurant Le Patalain in Marseille. —JF.

1½ cups sugar

1¼ cups water

2½ cups raspberries

1 tbsp lemon juice

6 cups fruit of choice (see note)

Sprigs fresh lemon balm (for garnish)

In a medium saucepan on medium-high heat, combine sugar and water and stir continually to dissolve sugar. Once sugar has dissolved, bring syrup to a boil, allowing it to boil for 1 minute (do no stir). Remove from heat to cool completely. In a blender or a food processor, combine 1½ cups raspberries, sugar syrup, and lemon juice and purée until smooth. Place a sieve over a bowl and strain mixture (discard what remains in sieve). In a glass bowl or among 4 dessert glasses, spoon some fruit, then top with raspberry mixture, then continue to add layers of fruit and raspberry mixture until used up. Garnish with lemon balm.

Makes 4 servings.

For the fruit, we like using a combination of whole blueberries, blackberries, raspberries, and red currants, halved and pitted cherries, and quartered strawberries.

Lemon balm is a herb that imparts a delightful lemon smell and flavor.

CLAFOUTIS WITH WHITE CHOCOLATE & MIXED BERRIES

....

For dessert at home, we often enjoy traditional cherry clafoutis, *which is a custard-based flan that originated in the Limousin region in central France. However, it's not the easiest dessert to serve in a busy restaurant because it's baked to order, so we adapted it to create a tarte with mixed local berries and white chocolate. We once took it off the menu but soon customers begged us to bring it back! This recipe will require an 8-in (20-cm) tarte pan which, in contrast to a pie pan, has a removable bottom and straight sides.*

TO PREPARE PASTRY SHELL: In a bowl, combine flour and sugar and cut in butter until butter resembles small peas. Make a hole in center of flour mixture and add egg and vanilla and mix until just combined. On a lightly floured surface, turn dough out and knead, adding water if needed. Return dough to bowl, cover in plastic wrap, and refrigerate for 1 hour. Remove from refrigerator and on a lightly floured surface, roll out dough into a circle then press down and with fingers to form a larger circle that will fit into tarte pan. Line an 8-in (20-cm) tarte pan with parchment paper. Carefully place dough in pan and form edges with fingers.

(continued)

PASTRY SHELL:

1 cup flour

¼ cup sugar

¼ cup cold butter

1 egg

½ tsp vanilla extract

1 tbsp water
(for kneading)

FILLING:

1 cup white chocolate, chopped

2 cups fresh or frozen mixed berries (e.g., raspberries, blackberries, blueberries, and/or strawberries)

1 cup whipping cream

7 tbsp butter

⅔ cup sugar

1 egg

¾ cups flour

TO PREPARE FILLING: Distribute chocolate and berries evenly on bottom of shell, carefully cover with plastic wrap, and refrigerate. In a stainless steel bowl or mixer, whip cream, then cover in plastic wrap and set aside in refrigerator. In a different or cleaned bowl of mixer, combine butter and sugar and whip on medium-high speed until well combined. Add egg and whip until light and fluffy and color changes from yellow to white. Stop mixer and add flour. On low speed, mix until just combined. Do not overmix. With a wooden spoon or rubber spatula, fold in pre-whipped cream.

Preheat oven to 350°F (180°C). Remove tarte pan from refrigerator, carefully uncover, and pour filling evenly over berries and chocolate. Place tarte pan on a baking sheet and bake 45 minutes or until golden brown. Remove from oven and let cool for 2 hours before serving.

MAKES 6 SERVINGS.

Torta di Capodanno

The *title of this recipe means "New Year's Cake" in Italian, but personally, I, being part-Italian, like making it during the summer, when all the fresh fruit is in season. Cherries and almonds are fabulous together. Serve warm with vanilla ice cream. This recipe requires an 8-in (20-cm) spring-form cheesecake pan.* —A.

1 cup + 2 tbsp unsalted butter

1⅓ cups sugar

3 eggs

1⅓ cups flour

1 tsp baking powder

1 tbsp butter (to coat sides of pan)

¾ cup sugar (for caramel)

½ cup sliced almonds

1 tsp vanilla extract

Fruit of choice, sliced or halved (see note)

Preheat oven to 350°F (180°C). With a hand blender or in a mixer on medium speed, cream together 1 cup + 2 tbsp butter and 1⅓ cups sugar. Mix in eggs, one at a time, incorporating after each one. Add flour and baking powder, reduce speed to low and mix until fluffy and well combined. Set mixture aside. Line bottom of a spring-form pan with parchment paper and use 1 tbsp butter to coat inner sides of pan. In a frying pan on medium-high heat, add ¾ cup sugar and heat for 8–10 minutes until it caramelizes and becomes a light cognac color—do not stir or the sugar will not caramelize. Pour into spring-form pan and sprinkle almonds evenly on top. Place fruit evenly to cover bottom and pour batter on top. Bake for about 1 hour, or until a skewer or fork inserted in center comes out clean.

Makes 6 servings.

You may use any fruit of choice for this torta, such as halved or sliced apricots, plums, peaches, pineapples, cherries, or pears. Just ensure you have enough fruit to cover the bottom of the pan.

RASPBERRY CRÈME BRÛLÉE

2¼ cups whipping cream

1 vanilla bean, split

2¼ cups half-and-half cream

⅔ cup sugar

3 whole eggs

8 egg yolks

1 cup raspberries

Warm water (to fill pan)

⅓ cup sugar (for caramelizing)

Fresh raspberries (for garnish)

A traditional crème brûlée *is much creamier than this recipe, but our version has always been well received due to the combination of raspberries and light custard. Don't be intimidated by the blowtorch, which are now readily available for the home cook at most kitchen supply shops. This recipe requires 8 ramekins, which are small, single-serving baking dishes often used for crème brûlée.*

Preheat oven to 300°F (150°C). In a heavy-bottomed pot on medium heat, combine whipping cream, vanilla bean, and half-and-half cream and bring just to a simmer. Meanwhile, in a large bowl, combine sugar, eggs, and egg yolks and whip until they turn a pale yellow color. Once cream is simmering, gently pour into egg mixture, and stir to combine. Place a sieve over a large bowl. Pour egg-cream mixture through sieve to remove any lumps (discard what remains in sieve). Evenly distribute raspberries into 8 ramekins, then crush berries into bottom. Pour strained crème brûlée mixture on top of raspberries, filling ramekins ¾ full. Place ramekins into a baking or roasting pan that is as tall as ramekins. Pour warm water into pan, until it reaches halfway up sides of ramekins. Cover pan with aluminium foil and bake for 45–50 minutes; the custards are done when they have minimal jiggle.

TO CARAMELIZE TOPS: Sprinkle each ramekin evenly with 2 tsp sugar. Light kitchen blowtorch. Hold torch about 2-in (5-cm) away from each ramekin to caramelize sugar, which should turn a light cognac color and form a hard crust. Garnish with raspberries.

MAKES 8 SERVINGS.

PEACH & WHITE CHOCOLATE BREAD PUDDING

This is a yummy and versatile dessert that you could also serve at breakfast. Instead of peaches, you can substitute with any seasonal berries, and instead of white chocolate, you can substitute with dark chocolate. Ideally, day-old croissants work best to absorb the milk. Serve with vanilla ice cream. This recipe requires a muffin pan for individual bread puddings or a 9×9-in (23×23-cm) square baking pan.

12 day-old croissants, cut into 1-in (2½-cm) cubes

1 cup sugar

1 can (13½-oz/400-mL) coconut milk

6 eggs

1 tbsp vanilla extract

2 cups sliced peaches

1 cup white chocolate, chopped

In a large bowl, combine croissants, sugar, coconut milk, eggs, and vanilla, cover in plastic wrap, and refrigerate for at least 2 hours (or overnight is best). Preheat oven to 325°F (165°C). Remove croissant mixture from refrigerator and add peaches and chocolate, and toss to combine. Line a muffin pan or lightly oil a 9×9-in (23×23-cm) square baking pan. Pour mixture evenly into liners or pan. Bake for 50–60 minutes, until golden brown.

MAKES 12 SERVINGS.

TRUFFLE CAKE

CRUST:

⅔ cup hazelnuts

⅔ cup sugar

⅓ cup flour

½ cup + 2 tbsp unsalted butter, softened

2¼ cups dark chocolate, chopped

1½ tbsp corn syrup

¾ cup unsalted butter, softened (for filling)

1¾ cups whipping cream

This is a quick and easy but very decadent dessert, which can be prepared a day in advance so you have more time to concentrate on your main meal. This recipe requires a 10-in (25-cm) cake pan.

TO PREPARE CRUST: Preheat oven to 350°F (180°C). In a food processor or mixer, combine hazelnuts, sugar, flour, and ½ cup + 2 tbsp butter and blend until mixture is smooth like peanut butter. In a 10-in (25-cm) cake pan with parchment paper, pour crust mixture evenly. Bake for 15–20 minutes, until golden brown.

Meanwhile, in a large bowl, combine chocolate, corn syrup, and ¾ cup butter and set aside. In a saucepan on medium-high, heat whipping cream until bubbles form on outer edges, then remove from heat and add to chocolate mixture. With a whisk, stir until mixture becomes smooth and silky. Once crust is finished baking, remove from oven, pour chocolate mixture into crust, and let it set for 4 hours (or overnight is best).

MAKES 10 SERVINGS.

Flambée Bananas

....

Once in a while our family will have a craving for this dessert. We usually have bananas readily available in the fruit basket, so it's a great dessert to whip up quickly. Serve with vanilla ice cream. This recipe requires a gas stove, or see note.

⅓ cup sugar

2 tbsp butter

4 bananas, sliced in half length-wise

2 tbsp rum

In a frying pan on a gas stove on high heat (or see note), combine sugar and butter and heat for 6–8 minutes, stirring continually, until butter starts to bubble. Add bananas flat-side down and cook for 2–3 minutes on each side. Remove pan from heat (but do not turn off heat) and pour rum over bananas. Return pan to heat carefully to ignite flames. Let alcohol burn off, then serve.

MAKES 4 SERVINGS.

THIS RECIPE WORKS WELL WITH PINEAPPLE SLICES IN PLACE OF BANANAS.

IF YOU DO NOT HAVE A GAS STOVE, YOU CAN USE AN ELECTRIC STOVE AND FLAMBÉ USING A MATCH LIT CLOSE TO THE PAN AFTER THE RUM IS ADDED.

Moist Chocolate Layer Cake

....

CAKE (best if prepared the night before):

2 cups puréed cooked beets (from 2 cans (14 oz/415 mL) beets, strained)

4¼ cups flour

4 tsp baking soda

4 tsp baking powder

3 cups + 2 tbsp tightly packed brown sugar

1 cup butter

6 eggs

1 cup buttermilk

1 tbsp vanilla extract

1½ cups melted dark chocolate

GANACHE:

3 cups whipping cream

4¼ cups dark chocolate, chopped into walnut-sized pieces

Every time Alessandra makes this cake, everyone is so impressed by its moistness. Little do they know that beets are what give this cake its richness and sweet flavor! Serve with raspberry coulis or Soupe aux Fruits Rouges (page 193). This recipe requires two 10-in (25-cm) cake pans. —JF.

Preheat oven to 350°F (180°C). In a food processor, finely purée beets (but do not liquefy) and set aside. In a large bowl, sift together flour, baking soda, and baking powder and set aside. In a separate bowl, using a hand blender or a mixer on medium speed, blend sugar and butter until butter becomes fluffy. Add eggs, buttermilk, and vanilla and mix batter to be well combined, scraping down sides of bowl as needed. Add flour mixture and 1½ cups melted chocolate. Reduce speed to low and mix until chocolate is just combined (do not overmix). Add puréed beets, increase speed to medium, and mix until beets are fully combined into mixture. Line two 10-in (25-cm) cake pans with parchment paper. Divide batter into pans. Bake for 30–40 minutes, until cake springs back upon touch or when a skewer or fork inserted in center comes out clean. Remove from oven and transfer cakes to a cooling rack, preferably overnight.

TO PREPARE GANACHE: In a heavy-bottomed pan on medium-high, heat whipping cream just until bubbles form on outer edges. In a large bowl, add chocolate pieces. Pour heated cream over chocolate and stir with a whisk until combined, with a silky texture. Let ganache cool completely before using.

Place 1 cake layer on a cake plate. With a rubber spatula, spread half ganache over cake and on sides. Place remaining cake layer on top and spread rest of ganache on top and along sides, smoothing all over.

MAKES ONE 2-LAYER CAKE; 10 SERVINGS.

GANACHE IS SIMPLY EQUAL PARTS CHOCOLATE AND WHIPPING CREAM MIXED TOGETHER; IT'S USED AS A DESSERT FILLING OR ICING, AS WELL AS FOR A BASE FOR TRUFFLES.

CHOCOLATE ESPRESSO POT DE CRÈME

....

Whenever we have chocolate-connoisseur guests visiting, this is the first dessert that we consider making for them. It's fast and easy and satisfies die-hard chocoholics. These pots de crème *are best served in small espresso cups (you will need 8–10 for this recipe), but if they are not available you can use shot glasses or small dessert wine glasses.*

In a large bowl, place chocolate and set aside. In a saucepan on medium-high heat, bring whipping cream just to a simmer for about 2 minutes, stirring continually, then stir in Kahlua and espresso and allow to heat through, then pour over chocolate. Let mixture sit for 1 minute, then stir until smooth. Add egg yolks and stir to combine. Add butter, 1 tbsp at a time, until completely incorporated into mixture. Pour evenly into 8–10 espresso cups and refrigerate for 2 hours.

MAKES 8–10 SERVINGS.

WHEN IN SEASON, PLACE CRUSHED RASPBERRIES IN BOTTOM OF EACH ESPRESSO CUP FOR AN ADDED TREAT.

1 cup + 2 tbsp good-quality dark chocolate, chopped small

1 cup whipping cream

3 tbsp Kahlua liqueur (or any liqueur of choice)

¼ cup brewed espresso

2 egg yolks

3 tbsp unsalted butter, room temperature

Crushed raspberries (see note)

Tiramisu

....

GANACHE:

2 cups dark chocolate, chopped

1 cup whipping cream

9 egg yolks

¼ cup Kahlua liqueur

1½ cups sugar

½ cup Marsala wine

1 lb (450 g) Mascarpone cheese

1 cup whipping cream

1 cup water

1 cup brewed espresso or very strong coffee

2 pkg (7-oz/200-g each) ladyfingers

2 tbsp cocoa powder (for garnish)

Not so French, but definitely one of our all-time favorite desserts. This recipe will please even the most discerning Italian! Serve with an espresso on the side for a pick-me-up in the afternoon. This recipe requires a 9×9-in (23×23-cm) baking pan.

TO PREPARE GANACHE: In a large bowl, add chocolate and set aside. In a heavy-bottomed saucepan on medium high, heat whipping cream until bubbles form on outer edges, then pour over chocolate and stir with a whisk until chocolate melts and mixture is smooth and silky. Set aside.

In a large pot on medium-high heat, add enough water to fill 2-in (5-cm) and bring to a boil. In a large stainless steel bowl, combine egg yolks, Kahlua, ½ cup sugar, and ¼ cup Marsala, and set over boiling water (this can also be done in a double boiler). Whisk mixture for about 5 minutes, until it stiffens, turns a pale yellow color, and has doubled in volume. Set aside to cool. In a mixer, cream Mascarpone cheese until it softens and texture is like whipped cream. In a separate bowl, add whipping cream and whip to form stiff peaks, then set aside. In a saucepan on high heat, combine 1 cup water and remaining 1 cup sugar and bring to a boil. Add espresso or coffee and remaining ¼ cup Marsala, stir to combine, then remove from heat and set aside.

Line a 9×9-in (23×23-cm) baking pan with plastic wrap. Fold creamed Mascarpone cheese into egg mixture and continue to fold until well combined. Fold whipped cream into egg mixture and continue to fold until well combined and fluffy. Soak each ladyfinger in coffee mixture, then transfer to pan; repeat until bottom of pan is covered with one layer of ladyfingers (do not overlap, and reserve remaining ladyfingers for second layer). Top with half of egg mixture and drizzle half of ganache all over. Repeat with a second layer of ladyfingers, and remaining egg mixture and ganache. Cover in plastic wrap and refrigerate overnight. Sprinkle with cocoa powder before serving.

Makes 8–10 servings.

LAVENDER & ORANGE CHEESECAKE WITH MIXED BERRY COMPOTE

CHEESECAKE:

¾ cups sugar

4 cups cream cheese

4 eggs

½ tsp lavender

¾ cup white chocolate, melted

1 tsp vanilla extract

2 tbsp Triple Sec liqueur

Rind of 1 orange (avoid white pith)

2½ cups graham cracker crumbs

⅓ cup melted butter

COMPOTE:

½ cup water

1 cup sugar

2 cups mixed berries of choice

1 cup sour cream (for garnish)

1 tbsp sugar (for garnish)

Cheesecake is not a typical Provençal dessert, but when I was growing up in Toronto, my mom used to make it all the time. Jean-Francis wasn't too keen when I suggested that we put it on Provence's menu, but when I added some lavender to the recipe, he quickly changed his mind! The sweetened sour cream is a delicious addition to finish off this perfect cheesecake. This recipe requires a 9-in (23-cm) spring-form pan. —A.

TO PREPARE CHEESECAKE: Preheat oven to 300°F (150°C). In a bowl or with a mixer, cream together sugar and cream cheese. Blend in eggs, one at a time, incorporating after each one is added. Stir in lavender, chocolate, vanilla, Triple Sec, and orange rind and continue to stir until well combined. In a bowl, combine graham cracker crumbs and melted butter and mix until well combined. In a 9-in (23-cm) spring-form pan, firmly pack graham cracker crumbs on bottom and sides. Pour cheese mixture into pan and bake for 45–60 minutes, until it begins to soufflé (puff up). Remove from oven, let cool, then cover and refrigerate for at least 4 hours (or overnight if possible).

TO PREPARE COMPOTE: In a saucepan on high, combine water and sugar and cook for 2 minutes, stirring continually, until sugar completely dissolves. Reduce heat to medium, add berries, and simmer for 12–15 minutes, stirring continually. Remove from heat, let cool, then refrigerate for 1 hour.

Before serving, in a bowl, mix together sour cream and 1 tbsp sugar. On each slice of cheesecake, top with compote and sweetened sour cream, or simply serve the compote and sweetened sour cream in bowls and let guests help themselves!

MAKES 10–12 SERVINGS.

AFTERWORD

....

Here is a recipe for love rather than food.

During our first year of dating, Jean-Francis and I took a vacation to Corsica with some friends, and each day we toured the island in search of the perfect beach. On one particularly beautiful day, our group found a spot that I thought was heaven on earth; we girls soaked up the sun while the boys went spear fishing for our evening meal. After a few hours in the intense Corsican sun, I needed to cool off. I swam out to a rock a short distance from the beach, climbed onto it, and quietly pondered the beauty around me. I turned and noticed Jean-Francis approaching me. He swam up and told me to wait while he dove back down. He quickly returned with a beautiful creature—*un oursin*—a sea urchin. Its large round body was covered with long black spines, which made me a little nervous. I knew that stepping on one could be very painful but Jean-Francis assured me that holding it gently would not cause it nor I any harm. I was amazed as I held the sea urchin in my hands, its spines slowly swaying back and forth. He then carefully took the creature from me, placed it beside me on the rock, and cut it open with the knife he conveniently had strapped around his ankle, then picked out the delicate orange meat with his knife and fed it to me. Now, I thought, forget about the beach being heavenly; this was the ultimate!

If you are lucky to find fresh sea urchin at your local seafood market, another simple way to enjoy it is spread on some French baguette with unsalted butter, with a refreshing glass of rosé. And don't forget to close your eyes and picture yourself sitting on a rock on a beautiful Corsican day being fed freshly caught sea urchin by a cute Frenchman; it will make it taste so much better! —*A.*

INDEX

....

NOTE: FOR RECIPE TITLES, ITALICIZED PAGE NUMBERS DENOTE LOCATION OF ACTUAL RECIPES.

PROVENCE
Mediterranean Grill

PROVENCE
marinaside

PROVENCE MEDITERRANEAN GRILL

4473 West 10th Avenue

Vancouver, BC, Canada

V6R 2H8

604.222.1980

PROVENCE MARINASIDE

1177 Marinaside Crescent

Vancouver, BC, Canada

V6Z 2Y3

604.681.4144

provencevancouver.com